SOUP

COOKBOOK

365 Days of Hearty Recipes to Keep You Cozy Year-Round | Discover the Freshest Ingredients for Irresistible Soups

Eloise Ruiz

Table of Contents

Introduction

"Welcome to the world of soups, where warmth, comfort, and nourishment collide in a delightful bowl. In this cookbook, we embark on a journey to explore the tantalizing flavors and aromatic wonders of soups from across the globe. From creamy bisques to hearty stews, we have curated the finest collection of recipes that are sure to warm your heart and tantalize your taste buds.

Our objective is to demystify the art of soup-making and empower both novice and seasoned chefs alike to embrace the joy of simmering pots and bold flavors. We believe that a well-crafted soup can serve as a canvas for culinary creativity, allowing endless possibilities for customization and personalization. Whether you prefer classic favorites or crave adventurous culinary experiments, this cookbook has something for everyone.

Dive into our carefully developed recipes that showcase the finest ingredients, innovative techniques, and heartwarming stories behind each creation. We have meticulously documented tips, tricks, and variations to guide you in your culinary endeavors. Each recipe is thoughtfully crafted to ensure a balance of flavors, textures, and nutritional benefits, making it suitable for every occasion and every palate.

From silky smooth soups that caress your taste buds to chunky, hearty broths that provide comfort in every spoonful, we invite you to embark on this culinary journey. Discover the joy of savoring a piping hot bowl of soup, prepared with love and served with care. Whether it's a cozy family dinner, an intimate gathering with friends, or a simple meal for yourself, our soup cookbook will be your trusted companion, inspiring you to create culinary magic with every simmer and slurp.

Join us as we delve into the captivating world of soups and unlock the secrets to creating culinary masterpieces that will warm your soul and nourish your body. Whether you're an experienced cook or just starting your culinary journey, " Souper Delights: A Collection Of Savory Soup Recipes " will empower you to create exquisite soups that will impress family and friends alike. Gather your ingredients, sharpen those knives, and get ready to embark on an epicurean expedition that will leave you craving more.

Chapter 1.   The Soup Enthusiast's Guide

Introduction to Soup Journey

Soup, a comforting and versatile dish, has been a part of human culinary traditions for centuries. From the ancient times to modern cuisine, soup has journeyed across cultures and evolved into a diverse category of dishes enjoyed worldwide. We will explore the fascinating history, cultural significance, and various types of soups prevalent in different regions.

The origins of soup can be traced back to prehistoric times when humans discovered the art of cooking. Early civilizations made soup by combining water, vegetables, and meat in a pot over an open fire. This simple preparation method allowed them to utilize available ingredients and create a filling and nourishing meal. As civilizations progressed, so did soup-making techniques. Greeks and Romans introduced more complex flavors with the addition of herbs and spices, while Chinese culture developed intricate broths and soups as a foundation of their cuisine.

Soup's journey continued as trade routes expanded and explorers voyaged across the globe. European explorers brought their soup-making traditions to the newly discovered continents, while African, Asian, and Indigenous American cultures shared their unique recipes. This cultural exchange infused soups with an array of flavors, ingredients, and cooking styles, leading to the formation of distinct regional soup cultures.

In Europe, soups like French Onion Soup, Italian Minestrone, and Hungarian Goulash gained popularity. These soups reflect the history and tastes of their respective regions, showcasing the diverse culinary heritage of the continent. Moving towards Asia, countries like Thailand, Vietnam, and Japan are renowned for their flavorful and aromatic soups such as Tom Yum, Pho, and Miso Soup. These soups are often influenced by the use of local spices, herbs, and traditional cooking techniques.

In the Americas, traditional soups like Mexican Tortilla Soup, Peruvian Quinoa Soup, and New England Clam Chowder showcase the rich cultural tapestry of the continent. Each soup is a reflection of the history and traditions of the indigenous tribes, colonial influences, and immigrant communities that shaped the region's culinary landscape.

As soup-making techniques evolved, specialized equipment like blenders, immersion blenders, and pressure cookers made it easier to create soups with various textures and flavors. Soups have evolved into a food suitable for a variety of diets and palates. Soups that adhere to dietary constraints such as being vegetarian, vegan, gluten-free, or dairy-free have become increasingly popular.

Beyond its culinary delights, soup often holds cultural significance within communities. It can be a symbol of comfort, celebration, or even healing. In many cultures, soups are shared during family gatherings, religious ceremonies, and important life events. They bring people together, fostering a sense of unity and connection.

To conclude, the journey of soup has been one of cultural exchange, innovation, and appreciation of ingredients. From humble beginnings to sophisticated creations, soup has embraced diversity and evolved in parallel with human civilization. Whether it's a classic family recipe or a contemporary fusion creation, soup continues to captivate our taste buds and nourish our bodies and souls. So, next time you savor a bowl of soup, take a moment to appreciate the rich journey it has undertaken throughout history.

Soup-Making Essentials

When it comes to making delicious and comforting soups, there are a few key essentials that every cook should have in their kitchen. These tools, ingredients, and techniques will help you create flavorful and nourishing soups that will warm your body and soul. Let's examine some of the basics for preparing soup:

1. Stock or broth:

A good soup starts with a flavorful base, and that's where stocks and broths come in. Whether you prefer chicken, vegetable, or beef-based soups, having a high-quality stock or broth on hand is crucial. You can make your own by simmering bones, vegetables, and aromatics for a long period of time, or you can purchase pre-made varieties from the store. Whichever option you choose, make sure to use stock or broth that is rich in flavor to enhance your soup.

2. A sturdy stockpot:

To make large batches of soup, you'll need a sturdy stockpot that can hold a significant amount of liquid. Look for a pot with a thick, heavy bottom to ensure even heat distribution and avoid scorching. A stockpot with a tight-fitting lid is also important to trap the heat and flavors inside.

3. A chef's sharp knife:

Making soup requires a chef's knife, like any other sort of cookery, to be in tip-top shape. You'll need to chop and dice vegetables, herbs, and meats, and a sharp knife will make this task easier and safer. Invest in a good quality chef's knife that feels comfortable in your hand and maintains its sharpness over time.

4. A reliable blender or immersion blender:

For smooth and creamy soups, a blender or immersion blender is a must. A countertop blender is ideal for pureeing large batches of soup, while an immersion blender is convenient for blending directly in the pot. Whichever option you choose, make sure it is powerful enough to blend even the toughest ingredients into a silky-smooth consistency.

5. A variety of aromatics and seasonings:

To enhance the flavors of your soups, it's important to have a variety of aromatics and seasonings on hand. These can include onions, garlic, ginger, herbs like bay leaves and thyme, spices like cumin or paprika, and salt and pepper. Experiment with different combinations to create soups with unique flavors that suit your taste preferences.

6. Fresh and seasonal ingredients:

Using fresh and seasonal ingredients will take your soups to the next level. Opt for ripe and juicy tomatoes in the summer, hearty root vegetables like carrots and potatoes in the winter, and vibrant greens in the spring. Fresh ingredients will not only add flavor but also ensure that your soups are packed with nutrients.

7. Patience and creativity:

Soup-making is a labor of love, requiring time and attention to detail. Patience is key when allowing flavors to develop and ingredients to simmer together. When it comes to preparing soup, you shouldn't be afraid to experiment with a wide variety of ingredients, flavors, and textures. Let your imagination guide you and have fun in the kitchen.

soup-making essentials include high-quality stocks or broths, a sturdy stockpot, a sharp chef's knife, a reliable blender or immersion blender, a variety of aromatics and seasonings, fresh and seasonal ingredients, and a combination of patience and creativity. With these tools and ingredients at your disposal, you'll be well-equipped to create delicious and comforting soups that will warm your heart and nourish your body. Enjoy!

Stocking Your Soup Pantry

To stock your soup pantry, it is important to have a variety of ingredients that can be used as a base for different types of soup. Here are some essential items to consider:

1. Broths and Stocks: Chicken, beef, vegetable, and seafood broth or stock is the foundation of many soup recipes. Having these on hand will ensure you have a flavorful base for your soups.

2. Canned Tomatoes: Both diced and crushed canned tomatoes can easily be incorporated into soups. They add depth and richness to the flavor profile.

3. Beans and Lentils: Stock up on canned or dried beans such as black beans, kidney beans, cannellini beans, and lentils. These are great sources of protein and can add substance to your soups.

4. Pasta and Rice: Having different types of pasta and rice in your pantry allows you to create a variety of soup recipes. From small macaroni noodles to long-grain rice, these ingredients help thicken and add texture to the soup.

5. Vegetables: Keep a selection of fresh and frozen vegetables like carrots, celery, onions, bell peppers, and leafy greens. These can be easily added to soups for added nutrition and flavor.

6. Herbs and Spices: A well-stocked spice rack is essential for creating flavorful soups. Common herbs and spices for soups include bay leaves, thyme, oregano, basil, cumin, paprika, and black pepper.

7. Condiments: Soy sauce, Worcestershire sauce, hot sauce, and other condiments can enhance the taste of your soups. These can be used to adjust the flavor according to your preference.

8. Additional Options: Depending on your preferences, you may want to add proteins like canned chicken, tofu, or cooked ground beef to your pantry. These proteins can be easily incorporated into various soup recipes.

Remember to store your pantry items in a cool, dry place with proper labeling and rotation to ensure freshness. By having these essential pantry items on hand, you can easily whip up a delicious and comforting bowl of soup whenever you crave one.

Chapter 2.   Classic Comforts

Chicken Noodle Soup: A Hug in a Bowl

Chicken noodle soup has long been recognized as a comforting and nourishing dish for individuals of all ages. It is often referred to as a "hug in a bowl," and for good reason. This popular soup is a great complement to any diet because of its delicious flavor and myriad health advantages.

One of the primary reasons why chicken noodle soup is considered important is its ability to alleviate cold and flu symptoms. Many of us have heard since an early age that eating a warm bowl of chicken noodle soup can help us feel better. This is not just an old wives' tale but has scientific backing. The warm broth soothes a sore throat and clears nasal congestion, while the chicken provides essential nutrients that aid in boosting the immune system.

Additionally, chicken noodle soup is a great source of hydration. When we're sick, it's common for our appetite and desire to drink fluids to decrease. However, consuming chicken noodle soup helps to replenish fluids in the body and prevent dehydration. The vegetables, such as carrots and celery, also contribute to the soup's hydration properties.

Not only is chicken noodle soup beneficial during illness, but it also serves as a comforting meal during times of emotional distress. The warmth and familiar flavors can provide a sense of comfort and security. Many people associate chicken noodle soup with memories of being cared for by loved ones, further enhancing its ability to provide emotional support.

Another important aspect of chicken noodle soup is its versatility. While the classic recipe usually includes chicken, noodles, and vegetables, it can be easily customized to fit individual preferences and dietary restrictions. Whether someone prefers to add extra spices for a kick of flavor or substitute the noodles for rice or gluten-free alternatives, chicken noodle soup can be adapted to suit a wide range of tastes and dietary needs.

chicken noodle soup is much more than just a delicious dish. It has become an iconic symbol of comfort and nourishment. Whether it's providing relief during illness or bringing comfort during difficult times, chicken noodle soup truly lives up to its reputation as a "hug in a bowl." Its ability to provide hydration, essential nutrients, and emotional support make it an indispensable part of our culinary repertoire. So, the next time you're feeling under the weather or in need of a warm embrace, reach for a bowl of chicken noodle soup and let its comforting qualities work their magic.

Tomato Basil Bliss: Homemade and Heartwarming

Tomato Basil Bliss: Homemade and Heartwarming is a delightful culinary creation that brings together the freshness of tomatoes and the aromatic flavors of basil. This dish is a testament to the beauty of homemade cooking and the comfort it brings to our hearts.

The importance of Tomato Basil Bliss lies in its simplicity and ability to evoke a sense of nostalgia. It is a dish that takes us back to our grandmother's kitchen, where the aroma of tomatoes simmering on the stove brings warmth and joy. The combination of ripe, juicy tomatoes and fragrant basil leaves creates a harmonious balance of flavors that is both comforting and refreshing.

One of the key factors that make Tomato Basil Bliss so special is the use of fresh, high-quality ingredients. By using the finest tomatoes and hand-picked basil, this dish is elevated to another level of taste and satisfaction. The tomatoes provide a burst of tanginess and sweetness, while the basil adds a hint of freshness and earthiness. Together, they create a harmonious symphony of flavors that dance on your taste buds.

Another reason for the importance of Tomato Basil Bliss is its versatility. This dish can be enjoyed in various forms, from a simple pasta sauce to a flavorful soup or a topping for bruschetta. It is a favorite of both home cooks and professional chefs because of its versatility, which enables limitless inventiveness in the kitchen.

Tomato Basil Bliss also offers a lot of health advantages. Tomatoes are an excellent source of vitamins A and C, in addition to other antioxidants. Additionally, they have anti-inflammatory qualities, which may help lower the chance of developing certain diseases. Basil, on the other hand, is packed with essential nutrients and has been used for centuries for its medicinal properties. It is believed to have antibacterial and anti-inflammatory effects, among other benefits.

In addition to its gastronomic and health benefits, Tomato Basil Bliss holds a special place in our hearts because of the memories and emotions it evokes. It is a dish that brings families together, encouraging shared meals and conversations around the dinner table. Its comforting aroma and delicious taste make it a favorite choice for gatherings and celebrations.

Tomato Basil Bliss: Homemade and Heartwarming is more than just a culinary creation – it is a symbol of homemade cooking and the love and care that goes into preparing a meal. Its simplicity, versatility, health benefits, and nostalgic charm make it an essential part of any kitchen. So next time you're in need of a heartwarming dish, turn to Tomato Basil Bliss and indulge in its homemade goodness.

Hearty Minestrone: Italian Comfort in a Pot

Traditional Italian soups like minestrone are renowned for their warmth and comfort. It is a flexible recipe that can be made into a nourishing and filling supper by adding different veggies, beans, and pasta. We will explore the importance of Hearty Minestrone as a culinary delight and highlight its benefits for both the body and the soul.

One of the key reasons why Hearty Minestrone holds such importance is its nutritional value. Packed with a wide range of vegetables like carrots, celery, onions, and tomatoes, this soup provides a rich source of essential vitamins and minerals. The combination of different vegetables ensures a diverse nutrient profile, making it a wholesome meal option. Beans, such as cannellini or kidney beans, are added for additional plant-based protein and fiber, making this a filling and satisfying option.

Another significant aspect of Hearty Minestrone is its ability to warm and comfort. As an Italian comfort food, it offers a sense of nostalgia and coziness. The aroma of simmering Minestrone, with its aromatic herbs and spices, can create a welcoming atmosphere that brings people together. It is a perfect dish for cold winter days or when one needs a comforting meal to lift their spirits.

Furthermore, Hearty Minestrone is an excellent choice for those following a vegetarian or vegan diet. Its plant-based ingredients make it a great protein alternative to meat-based soups. The combination of legumes and vegetables in Minestrone ensures a well-rounded meal that is both nutritious and delicious. It also provides an opportunity to experiment with different vegetables, allowing individuals to enjoy a variety of flavors and textures in one bowl.

In addition to being a healthy supper option, Hearty Minestrone is also quick and easy to prepare. With only one pot required for cooking, it minimizes the need for multiple pans and dishes. This makes it an ideal choice for individuals with busy schedules or those looking for a quick and easy meal. Moreover, leftovers can be stored and enjoyed later, making it a cost-effective and practical option.

Overall, Hearty Minestrone: Italian Comfort in a Pot is far more than just a bowl of soup. Its nutritional value, ability to warm and comfort, suitability for special diets, and convenience all contribute to its significance. Whether enjoyed as a standalone meal or as an appetizer, Hearty Minestrone is a versatile dish that brings both nourishment and happiness to those who savor it.

Chapter 3.   Healthy and Wholesome

Spicy Lentil and Sausage Soup: Satisfying and Nutritious

Spicy Lentil and Sausage Soup is a delightful and nourishing dish that combines the heartiness of lentils with the savoriness of sausage. In addition to satisfying your palate, this delectable soup offers important elements for a well-balanced diet.

One of the key reasons why Spicy Lentil and Sausage Soup is important is its high nutritional value. This soup's major component, lentils, is a very good source of protein as well as fiber and a variety of different vitamins and minerals. They are particularly high in manganese, iron, and folate. While fiber helps with digestion and fosters a sensation of fullness, protein is necessary for the development and repair of tissues. The combination of lentils and sausage in this soup ensures that you get a good balance of protein and flavor.

Moreover, Spicy Lentil and Sausage Soup is packed with other valuable nutrients. The vegetables added to the soup, such as carrots, celery, and onions, contribute to its nutritional profile. Carrots are an excellent source of vitamin A, while celery and onions provide antioxidants and other beneficial compounds. These ingredients enhance the soup's flavor and increase its health benefits.

Another important aspect of this soup is its spicy nature. The addition of spices, such as cayenne pepper or red chili flakes, not only adds a kick to the taste but also offers various health benefits. Spices like cayenne pepper can boost metabolism, aid digestion, and provide relief from inflammation. The heat from the spices can also promote sweating, helping to alleviate congestion during a cold or flu.

Spicy Lentil and Sausage Soup is a multifaceted dish that can be eaten in a variety of ways in addition to being nutritious. It can be had as a whole meal on its own, with crusty bread or a side salad. It can also be used as a base for other recipes, such as a sauce for pasta or a filling for stuffed vegetables. The flexibility of this soup allows for creativity in the kitchen and ensures that it can be enjoyed in different contexts.

Spicy Lentil and Sausage Soup is an important and delicious dish that offers both satisfaction and nourishment. Its combination of lentils, sausage, and spices provides a balance of protein, fiber, and other essential nutrients. Whether enjoyed as a standalone meal or used as a versatile ingredient, this soup is a testament to the importance of flavorful and nutritious dishes in a well-rounded diet.

Creamy Miso Soup with Tofu: Japanese Elegance

Creamy Miso Soup with Tofu is a beloved dish in Japanese cuisine, known for its delicate flavors and comforting qualities. This traditional soup has transcended its cultural boundaries and gained popularity worldwide. Its importance lies in its unique taste, nutritional value, and cultural significance.

One of the key ingredients in creamy miso soup is miso paste, which is made from fermented soybeans. This paste not only adds a distinct umami flavor to the soup but also provides beneficial probiotics for gut health. Additionally, miso paste contains essential minerals such as iron, calcium, and magnesium.

Another crucial component of the soup is tofu, a versatile and protein-rich ingredient commonly used in Japanese cuisine. Tofu absorbs the flavors of the soup, adding a silky texture to the dish. It is suitable for vegetarians and vegans because it is a wonderful source of plant-based protein. The combination of creamy miso paste and delicate tofu creates a harmonious balance of flavors. The soup is often garnished with scallions, seaweed, and sometimes mushrooms, enhancing its taste and visual appeal.

Apart from its delectable flavors and nutritional benefits, creamy miso soup with tofu holds significant cultural importance. In Japan, this soup is commonly served as part of a traditional breakfast or as a starter in meals. It is considered a comfort food that warms the soul and brings a sense of nostalgia.

Moreover, the preparation and serving of miso soup are steeped in Japanese etiquette and mindfulness. The art of making miso soup involves carefully balancing the flavors, proportions, and presentation to create a delightful culinary experience.

As a representation of Japanese elegance, creamy miso soup with tofu embodies the principles of simplicity, grace, and harmony. Its subtle flavors and smooth texture provide a soothing and nourishing experience. Whether enjoyed as a standalone dish or alongside other Japanese delicacies, this soup offers a unique and satisfying culinary journey.

creamy miso soup with tofu holds great importance due to its distinctive taste, nutritional value, and cultural significance. It is a testament to the elegance and sophistication of Japanese cuisine. With every sip, one can savor the rich flavors, experience the comfort it offers, and appreciate the artistry behind its creation.

Roasted Vegetable and Quinoa Soup: Nutrient-Packed Goodness

Roasted Vegetable and Quinoa Soup is a hearty, delicious meal that will please the entire family and can be made under 30 minutes! One of the healthiest foods on earth is soup, and this nutrient-rich soup recipe is amazing for you. This is a perfect meal for the colder months, which are quickly approaching.

To make this soup, you'll need cooked quinoa, which is a seed cooked like a grain. It is very healthy, containing iron, fiber, protein, and antioxidants. Quinoa is a complete protein source since it is one of the few plant foods that include enough levels of each of the nine essential amino acids. Although it may sound confusing, quinoa can be thought of as a fantastic protein complement to a vegan or vegetarian diet as well as a fantastic meat substitute.

Also on the ingredient list is the addition of various vegetables. The more the merrier, as the saying goes, as this increases the amount and array of vitamins, minerals, and antioxidants. To make this soup, begin by roasting the vegetables after coating them in olive oil. This enhances the flavor, and the vegetables become a little sweeter.

The first vegetable of choice is butternut squash, which contains a high dose of Vitamin A and is great for eyesight and boosting the immune system. Next up is the onion, which is a natural antioxidant and anti-inflammatory. After adding the onion, include the garlic, which boosts the immune system and aids in digestion. Finally, add the carrots, which are famously good for eyesight and are packed with Vitamin K, essential to building strong bones.

Including all of these ingredients will create a wonderful, filling soup with tons of health benefits and delicious flavor. Don't forget to season to taste!

Chapter 4. Veggie Delights

Spinach and White Bean Wonder: Greens Galore

Spinach and White Bean Wonder: Greens Galore is an important subject to discuss. It packs a punch in the nutritional value it carries in each serving, providing iron, fiber, potassium, and magnesium. Each component of this recipe is carefully considered for its rich contribution to an individual's recommended daily intake of nutrients.

The dish's main ingredient and primary source of nutrients is spinach, which also contains folate and the vitamins A, C, and K. A single intake of vitamin A has enough to maintain these processes for the entire day. Vitamin A is essential for vision and cellular regeneration. Vitamin K2 helps maintain bone health and vitamin C helps form collagen, which is important for the healing and repair of bodily tissue.

Vitamin C also supports a healthy immune system. Spinach contains fiber, which helps with digestion and keeps the gut in good shape. Folate is a crucial mineral for everyone since it helps with DNA synthesis and cell division.

The white beans provide protein and fiber and are an excellent source of iron, magnesium, and potassium, contributing to the overall nutritional value of the dish, making it a nutrient-dense and very healthy recipe. This dish provides the nutrients needed to maintain good health and support many of the body's essential processes.

The use of white beans and spinach in a dish results in a great flavor profile as well as a nutrient-dense meal that can be consumed either as the primary course or as an accompaniment to another meal. Spinach & White Bean Wonder is an important topic to discuss because of the nutritious ingredients included in this recipe.

Butternut Squash Elegance: Embracing Autumn's Bounty

Butternut squash elegance is a delightful expression of autumn's abundance. This humble yet versatile vegetable captivates our senses with its vibrant color, mild sweetness, and silky texture. Its importance extends far beyond mere culinary pleasure, as it embodies the essence of the fall season and offers numerous health benefits.

One of the key reasons for the importance of butternut squash elegance is its nutritional value. This vegetable is a nutritional powerhouse thanks to its abundance in important vitamins and minerals. With more than 100% of the daily recommended consumption in only one serving, it is a fantastic source of vitamin A. Vitamin A is essential for maintaining healthy vision, fortifying the immune system, and promoting the growth and development of cells. All of these benefits are made possible by vitamin A. Additionally, vitamin C, which is well known for its antioxidant effects, is abundant in butternut squash. Antioxidants are substances that protect the body from the damage that can be produced by potentially harmful free radicals. As a result, the chance of acquiring chronic illnesses such as coronary heart disease and some types of cancer is reduced. In addition, vitamin C is essential for the synthesis of collagen, which supports healthy skin, hair, and nails.

Butternut squash It is a good source of dietary fiber in addition to its nutrient content. In order to maintain a healthy digestive system, correct digestion, and constipation prevention, fiber is essential. Additionally, it assists in controlling blood sugar levels, lowering the risk of diabetes and enhancing general heart health.

Beyond its nutritional value, butternut squash elegance is a symbol of embracing autumn's bounty. As the leaves change color and the temperature drops, this vegetable brings warmth and comfort to our tables. It is a versatile ingredient in both savory and sweet recipes because of its naturally sweet flavor, which works wonderfully with a variety of spices.

Whether roasted, pureed, or added to soups, butternut squash elegance brings a touch of elegance and sophistication to any dish. Its velvety texture adds depth and richness, while its vibrant orange hue adds a pop of color to the plate. It complements a wide variety of ingredients, from earthy herbs like sage and thyme to bold flavors like cinnamon and nutmeg.

Moreover, butternut squash elegance supports local agriculture and sustainable food practices. It is a seasonal vegetable that may be farmed across the world, helping local farmers and lowering the environmental impact of long-distance travel. By choosing to incorporate this vegetable into our meals, we contribute to a more sustainable food system and promote a closer connection to our environment.

Turmeric Carrot Magic: A Golden, Healthy Soup

Turmeric Carrot Magic: A Golden, Healthy Soup is a delightful and nutritious dish that has gained much attention in recent years. Packed with numerous health benefits, this soup has become a favorite among health-conscious individuals. We will explore the importance of Turmeric Carrot Magic and its positive impact on our overall well-being.

One of the primary reasons for the importance of Turmeric Carrot Magic is the presence of its key ingredients – turmeric and carrots. The bright yellow spice known as turmeric is well known for its potent anti-inflammatory and antioxidant qualities. Curcumin, the primary active element in turmeric, has been the subject of an extensive amount of research into its potential health benefits. It aids in reducing inflammation, boosting the immune system, and promoting overall gut health.

However, carrots are a great source of fiber, antioxidants, and vital vitamins like A, C, and K. Consuming carrots can improve eyesight, support cardiovascular health, and contribute to radiant skin. When combined with the goodness of turmeric, carrots create a potent combination that can enhance the nutritional value of any meal.

The synergy between turmeric and carrots in Turmeric Carrot Magic creates a powerhouse of health benefits. Lack of frequent consumption of this soup has been related to chronic issues like heart disease, diabetes, and numerous types of cancer. The antioxidants present in turmeric and carrots help in fighting free radicals and protecting our cells from oxidative damage.

In addition to its health benefits, Turmeric Carrot Magic is also a culinary delight. The combination of turmeric's warm and earthy flavor with the slightly sweet taste of carrots makes for a delicious soup that can be liked by all age groups. It's a flexible recipe that can be altered to taste with the addition of other seasonings, herbs, or even coconut milk for a richer texture.

Moreover, Turmeric Carrot Magic is an excellent addition to a balanced diet. Its low-calorie content makes it suitable for those watching their weight while still providing a satisfying and nutritious meal. Whether enjoyed as a starter, a light lunch, or a comforting dinner, this golden soup offers a perfect balance of taste and health benefits.

Turmeric Carrot Magic: There are several reasons why a bowl of Golden, Healthy Soup should be a regular part of our diet. It harnesses the power of turmeric and carrots, two ingredients known for their nutritional value and positive impact on our well-being. Incorporating this soup into our regular meals can improve our overall health, support disease prevention, and provide a delicious and wholesome culinary experience. Turmeric Carrot Magic truly lives up to its name as a golden, healthy soup that nourishes both the body and the soul.

Chapter 5.   Cheesy Comforts

Kale and Chickpea Power Soup: Green Goodness with a Kick

Kale and Chickpea Power Soup: Green Goodness with a Kick is a highly nutritious and delicious soup that is packed with numerous health benefits. This soup is a great choice for anyone trying to increase their intake of greens because it is created with a variety of fresh kale, tasty chickpeas, and other ingredients.

One of the key highlights of Kale and Chickpea Power Soup is the use of kale as its main ingredient. Kale is considered a superfood due to its impressive nutrient profile. Along with minerals like calcium and iron, Vitamins A, C, and K can be found in decent quantities in it. In addition, kale has a lot of fiber and antioxidants, which help in reducing inflammation and promoting overall well-being.

Chickpeas, the other key component of this soup, offer a wealth of health advantages in addition to being an excellent resource for vegetarian protein. They include a lot of dietary fiber, which promotes good weight management and digestion. Chickpeas also contain beneficial minerals like manganese and folate, which are important for proper cell function and energy production.

The combination of kale and chickpeas in this soup creates a powerhouse of nutrients. It is an excellent choice for vegetarians and vegans as it provides a complete protein source and is low in saturated fats. Those who have a sensitivity to gluten can still enjoy this soup because it contains no wheat.

In addition to kale and chickpeas, Kale and Chickpea Power Soup includes various other ingredients that enhance its flavor and nutritional value. Common additions include onions, garlic, carrots, and spices like turmeric and cayenne pepper. These nutrients give dimension to the flavor, and they also provide health advantages like boosting the immune system and reducing inflammation.

The "Green Goodness with a Kick" part of the soup's name refers to the vibrant green color and the subtle spiciness that it offers. The kick comes from the addition of spices that add a bit of heat to the soup, making it an exciting and flavorful choice.

Overall, Kale and Chickpea Power Soup: Green Goodness with a Kick is not only a tasty and satisfying meal but also a nourishing option for those looking to improve their diet. Its combination of kale, chickpeas, and other nutritious ingredients provides a wealth of health benefits and ensures a well-balanced meal. So, this soup is unquestionably worthwhile to try whether you're a health-conscious person or simply trying to include more greens in your diet.

Creamy Broccoli Cheddar Bliss: The Perfect Pairing

Creamy Broccoli Cheddar Bliss is a delectable combination of flavors that has gained immense popularity among food enthusiasts. This dish is a testament to the fantastic pairing of broccoli and cheddar cheese, creating a culinary experience that is truly unforgettable.

The importance of Creamy Broccoli Cheddar Bliss lies not only in its tantalizing taste but also in its nutritional value. Broccoli, a cruciferous vegetable, is packed with essential vitamins and minerals. Broccoli contains essential minerals like vitamin C, vitamin K, and folate that support healthy blood clotting and a strong immune system.; it is also high in fiber, which supports in digestion; and it is a fantastic source of antioxidants, which support overall health.

Cheddar cheese, on the other hand, adds a creamy and savory element to this dish. Calcium is a necessary mineral for strong bones and teeth, and this food is an excellent supply of calcium in concentrated form. Cheddar cheese also provides a good amount of protein, making Creamy Broccoli Cheddar Bliss a satisfying and nutritious meal option.

The combination of these two ingredients in Creamy Broccoli Cheddar Bliss creates a harmonious blend of flavors. The creaminess of the cheddar cheese balances out the slight bitterness of the broccoli, resulting in a taste that is both comforting and indulgent. The warmth and richness of this dish make it a perfect choice for cool evenings or as a hearty side dish.

Moreover, this pairing offers a versatile base for additional ingredients and variations. For those who enjoy an extra kick, adding some diced jalapenos or a sprinkle of red pepper flakes can elevate the flavor profile. Alternatively, incorporating cooked bacon or grilled chicken can provide a protein boost and add a smoky essence to the dish. The possibilities are endless, allowing individuals to customize Creamy Broccoli Cheddar Bliss to their own preferences.

Creamy Broccoli Cheddar Bliss is more than just a dish; it is a testament to the perfect pairing of broccoli and cheddar cheese. Its nutritional value, exquisite taste, and versatility make it an important addition to any menu. Whether enjoyed on its own or as part of a larger meal, this delightful dish will continue to captivate taste buds and leave a lasting impression.

Kid-Friendly Alphabet Soup: Fun and Nutritious

Kid-Friendly Alphabet Soup is a fun and nutritious option for kids of all ages. This kind of soup has numerous advantages that support a child's general growth in addition to making a delicious and enjoyable meal. One of the key advantages of Kid-Friendly Alphabet Soup is its ability to introduce young children to the alphabet in an interactive and engaging way. The soup contains pasta shapes in the form of letters, allowing kids to identify and become familiar with different letters while they eat. This can significantly enhance their literacy skills and make the learning process more enjoyable.

Furthermore, Kid-Friendly Alphabet Soup is typically packed with nutritious ingredients, including vegetables and lean proteins. This makes it a healthier alternative to other types of soups that may contain higher levels of sodium and unhealthy additives. By incorporating vegetables into the soup, children can receive essential vitamins and minerals necessary for their growth and development.

In addition, the fun and interactive nature of Kid-Friendly Alphabet Soup can also encourage fussy eaters to try new ingredients. The colorful pasta shapes and the excitement of finding different letters can make the mealtime experience more enjoyable and less intimidating for picky eaters. This can, in turn, help broaden their palate and increase their willingness to try new foods.

Kid-Friendly Alphabet Soup can also offer a shared experience between parents and their children. Enjoying a bowl of alphabet soup together provides an opportunity for bonding and learning. Parents can engage in conversations with their kids about the letters they find, spelling simple words, or even creating stories using the letters as a starting point. This can help strengthen family relationships and create positive associations with mealtime.

Kid-Friendly Alphabet Soup is not only a fun and enjoyable meal option for children but also provides numerous benefits. From promoting literacy skills to introducing nutritious ingredients, this type of soup can play a significant role in a child's development. By incorporating Kid-Friendly Alphabet Soup into mealtime routines, parents can foster a love for learning, encourage healthier eating habits, and create meaningful connections with their children.

Chapter 6. International Inspirations

Pasta e Fagioli Italiano: A Taste of Italy

Pasta e Fagioli Italiano, also known as pasta and beans, is a traditional Italian dish that holds great importance in Italian cuisine. This hearty and flavorful dish has been a staple in Italian households for centuries, and it has also gained popularity worldwide for its taste and nutritional value.

One of the main reasons why Pasta e Fagioli Italiano is highly regarded is its simplicity. The dish consists of basic ingredients such as pasta, beans, tomatoes, onions, garlic, and herbs. These ingredients are readily available in most kitchens, and the recipe is easy to follow, making it accessible to anyone who wants to enjoy a taste of Italy.

The importance of this dish lies not only in its simplicity but also in its versatility. Pasta e Fagioli Italiano can be easily modified to suit individual tastes and preferences. Some variations include adding bacon or sausage for a meatier texture, while others prefer to keep it vegetarian. This adaptability allows people to personalize the dish while still keeping its essence intact.

Apart from its delicious taste, Pasta e Fagioli Italiano is also highly nutritious. The combination of pasta and beans provides a good amount of protein, carbohydrates, and fiber, making it a well-rounded meal. The beans, whether they are cannellini, borlotti, or kidney beans, offer numerous health benefits, including promoting heart health and regulating blood sugar levels.

The cultural significance of this dish is another reason why it is important in Italian cuisine. Pasta e Fagioli Italiano is deeply rooted in Italian traditions and is often enjoyed during the winter months when warm and comforting meals are craved. It is a dish that brings families together, as it is often prepared and shared during gatherings and celebrations.

Furthermore, Pasta e Fagioli Italiano showcases the essence of Italian cooking, which emphasizes the use of fresh and seasonal ingredients. The flavors of the dish are enhanced by the quality and freshness of the ingredients used, making it a true representation of Italian culinary heritage.

Pasta e Fagioli Italiano holds great importance as a traditional Italian dish that embodies the simplicity, versatility, and nutritional value that Italian cuisine is known for. Whether enjoyed on a cold winter day or at a festive gathering, this dish brings people together through its delicious taste and cultural significance. It is truly a taste of Italy that is cherished both in Italy and around the world.

Sweet Potato and Apple Surprise: A Sweet and Savory Blend

Sweet Potato and Apple Surprise is a delightful dish that combines the sweetness of apples with the earthy flavors of sweet potatoes. This unique blend creates a mouthwatering taste experience that satisfies both sweet and savory cravings. We will explore the importance of this delicious dish and why it should be a part of everyone's culinary repertoire.

One of the key reasons why Sweet Potato and Apple Surprise is important is its nutritional value. Vitamin and mineral content is high in both sweet potatoes and apples. Beta-carotene, vitamin C, and fiber are abundant in sweet potatoes, and antioxidants, fiber, and vitamins are plentiful in apples. By combining these two ingredients, you not only enhance the taste but also increase the nutritional benefits of the dish.

Furthermore, Sweet Potato and Apple Surprise offers a unique flavor profile that is both comforting and impressive. The natural sweetness of apples complements the natural sweetness of sweet potatoes, creating a harmonious balance. The savory notes from herbs and spices add depth to the dish, making it a memorable and sophisticated culinary experience. Even picky eaters will love this flavorful combination, which works equally well as an accompaniment or main course.

Another reason why Sweet Potato and Apple Surprise is important is its versatility. This dish can be enjoyed in various ways, allowing for creativity in the kitchen. It can be baked, roasted, mashed, or even turned into a soup. The possibilities are endless, and you can customize it according to your preferences and dietary needs. The versatility of this dish makes it suitable for any occasion, whether it's a family dinner, a holiday feast, or a casual gathering.

In addition, the combination of sweet potatoes and apples in this dish showcases the potential of pairing contrasting flavors. The sweetness of the apples helps to balance the earthy sweetness of the sweet potatoes, resulting in a well-rounded and satisfying taste. This is a testament to the power of culinary exploration and the endless possibilities that can arise from experimenting with different ingredients.

Sweet Potato and Apple Surprise also holds cultural significance in some regions. In certain cuisines, these ingredients are commonly used together to create traditional dishes that have been passed down through generations. By appreciating and embracing these culinary traditions, we not only celebrate diversity but also preserve our cultural heritage.

Sweet Potato and Apple Surprise is not just a delicious dish but also an important blend of flavors. Its nutritional value, unique taste profile, versatility, and cultural significance make it a dish worth exploring and embracing. So, next time you're in the kitchen, consider whipping up this delightful creation and indulge in the sweet and savory goodness it has to offer.

Creamy Tomato Mac 'n' Cheese Soup: Childhood Reimagined

the nostalgia of childhood with a modern twist. This unique soup takes the classic macaroni and cheese and transforms it into a creamy tomato-based soup that will warm your soul.

One of the reasons why Creamy Tomato Mac 'n' Cheese Soup is so important is that it brings back memories of childhood. Macaroni and cheese was a staple in many of our childhoods. We found happiness and warmth in the ease and simplicity of the meal. This soup combines that nostalgia with the flavors of creamy tomato soup, creating a dish that takes us back to our childhood while also giving it a new and exciting twist.

Another reason why this soup is important is its versatility. Creamy Tomato Mac 'n' Cheese Soup can be enjoyed as a meal on its own or paired with crusty bread or a side salad. It can also be customized by adding ingredients like cooked bacon, sautéed mushrooms, or chopped fresh herbs, allowing you to create your own unique version of this dish. The possibilities are endless, and you can truly make it your own.

In addition to its delicious taste and versatility, Creamy Tomato Mac 'n' Cheese Soup also offers nutritional benefits. The combination of tomatoes and cheese provides a good source of vitamins, minerals, and antioxidants. Tomatoes are rich in vitamin C, potassium, and lycopene, which is known for its health benefits. Cheese has both calcium and protein, two essential nutrients. By enjoying this soup, you can indulge in comfort food while also nourishing your body.

Lastly, the importance of Creamy Tomato Mac 'n' Cheese Soup lies in its ability to bring people together. It is a dish that can be shared with family and friends, creating memories and fostering connections. Whether it's a cozy family dinner or a gathering with loved ones, this soup has the power to bring people closer and create moments of joy.

Creamy Tomato Mac 'n' Cheese Soup: Childhood Reimagined, is a dish that holds immense importance. It combines the nostalgia of childhood with a modern twist, offering a delicious, versatile, and nutritious option. Whether you are looking to relive your childhood memories or create new ones, this soup is an excellent choice. So go ahead, indulge in a bowl of Creamy Tomato Mac 'n' Cheese Soup and reimagine your childhood through its comforting flavors.

Chapter 7.   Meaty Marvels

Beef Stew Perfection: Hearty and Fulfilling

Beef stew perfection is more than just a dish; it is a culinary masterpiece that embodies comfort and satisfaction. This hearty and fulfilling delicacy has been cherished by people across cultures for centuries. Its significance lies not only in its delicious taste but also in its ability to bring people together and evoke a sense of nostalgia.

First and foremost, beef stew perfection is known for its rich and robust flavors. The slow cooking method allows the flavors of the beef, vegetables, and herbs to meld together, creating a symphony of tastes that delights the palate. The tender chunks of beef, vegetables like potatoes, carrots, and onions, and the aromatic herbs like thyme and bay leaves combine harmoniously to create a dish that is deeply satisfying.

Beyond its taste, beef stew is a symbol of warmth and comfort. During colder months, a bowl of hot beef stew can offer solace and coziness. It warms the body and nourishes the soul. The steam rising from the bowl, the aroma filling the room, and the sight of the succulent beef and vegetables create a sensory experience that is unparalleled. It brings back fond memories of family gatherings, where conversations flowed freely and the comforting aroma of beef stew filled the air.

Furthermore, beef stew perfection is a flexible recipe that can be altered to meet the needs of a variety of diets and food preferences. Whether you prefer a classic beef stew or want to add your own twist by incorporating additional ingredients or spices, the possibilities are endless. From adding red wine for depth of flavor to experimenting with alternative protein sources like chicken or lamb, beef stew can be adapted to cater to various tastes and dietary needs.

From a nutritional standpoint, beef stew is a well-balanced meal that provides essential nutrients. It is packed with protein from the beef, vitamins and minerals from the vegetables, and healthy fats from the broth. The combination of these elements makes beef stew not only delicious but also a nourishing option for those seeking a fulfilling and wholesome meal.

beef stew perfection is a dish that goes beyond mere sustenance. It represents a medley of flavors, a source of comfort, and an opportunity for customization. Whether enjoyed on a cold winter day or shared with loved ones, beef stew holds a special place in the culinary world. It encompasses the heartiness and fulfillment that only a truly exceptional dish can offer.

Thai Coconut Curry Adventure: Aromatic and Spicy

Thai coconut curry has become quite well-known all over the world. It is known for its distinct flavors and aromatic spices. The combination of coconut milk, curry paste, and a variety of vegetables and proteins creates a symphony of flavors that tantalize the taste buds.

One of the main reasons Thai coconut curry is highly regarded is its unique blend of spices. The curry paste, which usually consists of ingredients such as lemongrass, galangal, garlic, shallots, and a fragrant herbs and spices, which give the dish more nuance and richness. Each ingredient plays a crucial role in creating a balanced and flavorful curry.

The use of coconut milk as a base adds richness and creaminess to the curry, giving it a velvety texture. Coconut milk tames the spiciness of the curry paste and provides a pleasant contrast to the heat. The combination of the aromatic spices and coconut milk creates a harmonious flavor profile that is both satisfying and addictive.

Thai coconut curry also offers a wide variety of customization. It can be made with different proteins such as chicken, shrimp, beef, or tofu, making it suitable for omnivores and vegetarians alike. Additionally, a variety of vegetables like bell peppers, broccoli, and bamboo shoots can be added to enhance the nutritional value and taste of the dish.

The importance of Thai coconut curry adventure extends beyond its delectable taste. It is a dish that brings people together, allowing them to share a communal dining experience. Whether enjoyed at a Thai restaurant or prepared at home, Thai coconut curry becomes a centerpiece, evoking a sense of celebration and togetherness.

Moreover, Thai coconut curry is known for its health benefits. Coconut milk is full of medium-chain fatty acids, a type of fatty acid that is simple for the body to process and that can give a rapid source of energy. The abundance of vegetables in the dish ensures a good intake of vitamins, minerals, and dietary fiber. The combination of proteins and vegetables results in a nutritious, well-rounded meal.

Thai coconut curry adventure is not just a dish; it is a gastronomic journey that stimulates the senses and brings people together. Its unique blend of spices, creamy coconut milk, and versatile ingredients make it a flavor-packed experience. Whether you are a spice lover or someone who appreciates a well-balanced meal, Your taste buds will be delighted with Thai coconut curry and you'll want more. So go ahead, embark on a Thai coconut curry adventure, and discover the aromatic and spicy wonders it has to offer!

Creamy New England Clam Chowder: From the Coast to Your Bowl

Creamy New England Clam Chowder is a beloved dish that has been enjoyed by seafood lovers for generations. It is a soup that originates from the New England region of the United States, particularly from the coastal areas where clams are abundant. This aims to discuss the importance of Creamy New England Clam Chowder and why it has become a staple in culinary culture.

One of the primary reasons for the significance of Creamy New England Clam Chowder is its rich and indulgent taste. The soup is made with fresh clams, potatoes, onions, and often includes bacon for added flavor. The combination of these ingredients creates a smooth and velvety texture that is both satisfying and comforting. The creaminess of the soup balances perfectly with the briny and slightly sweet taste of clams, resulting in a harmonious blend of flavors.

Furthermore, Creamy New England Clam Chowder showcases the freshness and abundance of seafood in the New England region. The dish is a celebration of regional ingredients, particularly the locally sourced clams. The clams used in the soup are typically harvested from the nearby coastal waters, ensuring their freshness and quality. By highlighting the local seafood, Creamy New England Clam Chowder reinforces the importance of supporting sustainable and local food sources.

Another aspect that makes Creamy New England Clam Chowder significant is its versatility. While traditionally served as a soup, it can also be adapted into various dishes. The thick and creamy base of the chowder can be used as a sauce for seafood pasta or incorporated into seafood pot pie. This adaptability expands the culinary possibilities and allows for creativity in the kitchen.

Creamy New England Clam Chowder also holds a cultural significance in the New England region. It is considered a comfort food and is often associated with memories of cozy family gatherings or enjoying a warm bowl on a chilly coastal evening. The soup has become deeply ingrained in the culinary traditions of the area, representing the region's rich history and heritage.

Creamy New England Clam Chowder holds great importance both gastronomically and culturally. Its rich and indulgent taste, utilization of fresh seafood, versatility, and cultural significance have propelled it to become a beloved dish throughout the New England region. Whether enjoyed by locals or visitors, this iconic soup is a testament to the culinary excellence of the coastal areas and continues to bring joy to countless individuals.

Chapter 8.   Broth Basics

Homemade Chicken Stock Base: The Foundation of Great Soup

Homemade chicken stock base is the foundation of great soup due to its numerous benefits. Firstly, homemade chicken stock base enhances the flavor of the soup and adds depth to it. The combination of chicken bones, vegetables, and aromatic herbs creates a rich and savory taste that store-bought stocks cannot replicate.

Additionally, homemade chicken stock base is highly nutritious. It contains essential nutrients, such as collagen, vitamins, and minerals, which are released during the simmering process. These nutrients contribute to the overall health benefits of the soup and help boost the immune system.

Moreover, homemade chicken stock base allows for customization and control over the ingredients. Unlike store-bought options that may contain additives, preservatives, and excessive sodium, making your own stock allows you to choose quality ingredients and adjust the seasonings according to your preference. This ensures a healthier and more tailored soup.

Furthermore, using homemade chicken stock base supports sustainable cooking practices. It encourages the utilization of leftover chicken bones and vegetable scraps, reducing food waste in the process. By repurposing these ingredients, you contribute to environmental sustainability and reduce your ecological footprint.

homemade chicken stock base is the foundation of great soup due to its enhanced flavor, nutritional value, customization options, and support for sustainable cooking. It elevates the taste and quality of soups while providing numerous health benefits. Incorporating homemade chicken stock base into your cooking repertoire is a worthwhile endeavor that will greatly enhance your soup-making skills.

Vegan Lentil and Veggie Feast: Plant-Based Goodness

The Vegan Lentil and Veggie Feast: Plant-Based Goodness is a delightful and nutritious plant-based meal that is perfect for vegans and anyone looking to incorporate more plant-based options into their diet. This feast consists of a variety of dishes made with lentils and assorted vegetables, offering a burst of flavors, textures, and nutrients.

One of the highlights of this feast is the lentil soup, a hearty and satisfying dish that serves as a great starter. Made with wholesome ingredients such as lentils, onions, carrots, celery, and a flavorful vegetable broth, this soup is packed with protein, fiber, and essential vitamins and minerals. The lentils add a creamy and slightly earthy taste, while the vegetables provide a refreshing crunch.

Moving on to the main course, the Vegan Lentil and Veggie Feast offers a mouthwatering lentil and vegetable stir-fry. This dish combines cooked lentils with a medley of fresh vegetables like bell peppers, broccoli, zucchini, and mushrooms. The stir-fry is seasoned with a delectable blend of herbs and spices, enhancing the natural flavors of the ingredients. It is a perfect balance of textures with tender lentils and crispy vegetables.

Accompanying the stir-fry are aromatic basmati rice and a vibrant mixed green salad. The basmati rice adds a fragrant element to the meal, while the mixed green salad provides freshness and crunch. The salad can be dressed with a light vinaigrette or a creamy vegan dressing of your choice.

To top it all off, a delectable vegan dessert is included in this feast. Options may vary, but some popular choices include a rich and creamy vegan chocolate mousse or a refreshing fruit salad with a drizzle of maple syrup.

The Vegan Lentil and Veggie Feast: Plant-Based Goodness not only satisfies your taste buds but also nourishes your body with essential nutrients. By opting for this plant-based feast, you can enjoy a delicious and wholesome meal that supports your health and aligns with your dietary preferences.

Please note that the exact recipes and ingredients may vary, so it's best to refer to specific recipes or consult a professional chef for further details. Enjoy your Vegan Lentil and Veggie Feast and embrace the plant-based goodness!

Low-Sodium Minestrone Bliss: Heart-Healthy Flavor

Minestrone Bliss is a delicious and nutritious low-sodium soup option that offers heart-healthy flavor. This will explore the importance of Low-Sodium Minestrone Bliss and its impact on our overall well-being.

First and foremost, reducing sodium intake is crucial for maintaining a healthy heart. High sodium consumption has been associated with increased blood pressure, which can contribute to heart disease and other cardiovascular conditions. By opting for low-sodium alternatives like Minestrone Bliss, individuals can enjoy a flavorful meal while promoting heart health.

Minestrone Bliss is carefully crafted to include wholesome ingredients that not only enhance taste but also provide essential nutrients. Packed with a variety of vegetables, such as carrots, celery, tomatoes, and zucchini, this soup offers a wide range of vitamins, minerals, and dietary fiber. These nutrients are crucial for supporting overall health, including heart function.

Furthermore, Low-Sodium Minestrone Bliss is a great option for individuals looking to manage their weight. Its low-calorie content combined with the high water and fiber content helps promote feelings of fullness, preventing overeating. Maintaining a healthy weight is essential for reducing the risk of heart disease and other chronic conditions.

In addition to its heart-healthy benefits, Minestrone Bliss offers a flavorful and satisfying experience. With the right blend of seasonings, herbs, and spices, this soup tantalizes taste buds, making it appealing to individuals seeking a delicious meal option. By choosing Low-Sodium Minestrone Bliss, individuals can enjoy a flavorful and nourishing meal without compromising their health.

Moreover, Minestrone Bliss can be easily incorporated into a balanced diet. It can serve as a nourishing and satisfying main meal or a hearty and comforting side dish. Its versatility allows individuals to customize their meals according to their preferences and dietary needs.

Low-Sodium Minestrone Bliss embodies the importance of heart-healthy flavor. By choosing this delicious soup, individuals can maintain a healthy heart, nourish their bodies with essential nutrients, manage their weight, and indulge in a flavorful culinary experience. With its wholesome ingredients and robust flavor profile, Minestrone Bliss is an excellent option for those looking to prioritize their heart health without compromising on taste.

Chapter 9.   Dietary Delights

Dairy-Free Creamy Tomato Magic: Lactose-Intolerant Friendly

Dairy-free creamy tomato magic is a delightful culinary creation that caters to individuals who are lactose intolerant. It offers a rich and velvety texture, combined with the vibrant flavors of tomato, to provide a delectable experience without any digestive discomfort.

One of the key reasons why dairy-free creamy tomato magic holds immense importance is its ability to accommodate the dietary needs of those who are lactose intolerant. Lactose intolerance is a condition where the body is unable to digest lactose, the sugar found in milk and other dairy products. Consuming dairy can lead to various uncomfortable symptoms such as gas, bloating, and diarrhea for lactose-intolerant individuals. Thus, having a dairy-free alternative like creamy tomato magic ensures that such individuals can enjoy a delicious and creamy dish without worrying about adverse health effects.

Not only does dairy-free creamy tomato magic fulfill a specific dietary requirement, but it also offers numerous health benefits. Tomatoes, the main ingredient of this culinary creation, are a rich source of various vitamins, minerals, and antioxidants. They are packed with vitamin C, vitamin A, potassium, and lycopene, which contribute to improved immune function, healthy skin, and the prevention of certain diseases. By incorporating tomatoes into a creamy and lactose-free base, creamy tomato magic provides a nutritious option that promotes overall well-being.

Furthermore, dairy-free creamy tomato magic opens up new culinary possibilities for lactose-intolerant individuals. It can be used as a versatile ingredient in a variety of dishes, ranging from classic pastas and pizzas to creative soups and sauces. Its creamy texture and tangy tomato flavor can bring depth and richness to any recipe while remaining safe for those with lactose intolerance. This allows individuals to explore an extensive range of flavors and enjoy a diverse array of meals, making their dining experiences more enjoyable and satisfying.

In addition to its dietary and health benefits, dairy-free creamy tomato magic also promotes inclusivity and accessibility in the culinary world. It ensures that lactose-intolerant individuals can partake in shared dining experiences without feeling left out or compromising on their dietary needs. By offering a delectable alternative that mirrors the creaminess of traditional dairy-based dishes, it fosters a sense of inclusiveness and allows everyone to enjoy a similar gastronomic experience.

dairy-free creamy tomato magic holds great importance, particularly for individuals who are lactose intolerant. It provides a delectable and creamy option that caters to their dietary requirements, eliminates digestive discomfort, and offers numerous health benefits. Moreover, it opens up culinary possibilities, promotes inclusivity, and allows for shared dining experiences. With its unique combination of flavors and textures, dairy-free creamy tomato magic truly lives up to its name – a magical creation that brings joy and satisfaction to lactose-intolerant individuals.

Paleo Butternut Squash Delight: A Caveman's Soup

The importance of Paleo Butternut Squash Delight: A Caveman's Soup lies in its nutritious and delicious nature. This soup combines the goodness of butternut squash with other paleo-friendly ingredients to create a hearty and fulfilling dish that is perfect for a caveman's diet.

First and foremost, butternut squash is a nutrient powerhouse. It is rich in vitamins A, C, and E, as well as potassium, magnesium, and dietary fiber. These nutrients contribute to a healthy immune system, eye health, and overall well-being. By incorporating butternut squash into a soup, you can easily and deliciously reap the benefits of this superfood.

Furthermore, Paleo Butternut Squash Delight is made using only paleo-approved ingredients. The Paleo diet emphasizes whole, unprocessed foods that our ancestors would have eaten during the Paleolithic era. By following this diet, individuals can avoid processed sugars, grains, and dairy while consuming lean proteins, healthy fats, and plenty of fruits and vegetables. This soup aligns perfectly with those principles, making it an ideal choice for someone following a Paleo lifestyle.

In addition to its nutritional value and adherence to the Paleo diet, Paleo Butternut Squash Delight offers a unique and comforting taste. The combination of earthy butternut squash, savory herbs, and aromatic spices creates a flavor profile that is both satisfying and nostalgic. Enjoying a bowl of this soup can transport you to a simpler time, evoking a sense of connection with our ancestral roots.

Overall, the importance of Paleo Butternut Squash Delight: A Caveman's Soup lies in its ability to provide a nutrient-dense, Paleo-friendly, and delicious meal option. Whether you are following a Paleo lifestyle or simply looking for a nourishing and flavorful dish, this soup is a fantastic choice. Incorporate it into your diet and experience the benefits that come with enjoying a caveman's favorite soup. Enjoy!

Gluten-Free Chicken and Rice Comfort: For Those with Sensitivities

Gluten-free diets have become increasingly popular in recent years, particularly among individuals with gluten sensitivities or intolerances. For those who find comfort in classic comfort foods like chicken and rice, it is essential to find gluten-free options that can provide the same level of satisfaction. This will explore the significance of gluten-free chicken and rice comfort meals for those with sensitivities.

First and foremost, it is important to understand the impact of gluten on individuals with sensitivities. Gluten is a protein found in wheat, barley, and rye, which can trigger adverse symptoms in those with gluten-related disorders such as celiac disease or non-celiac gluten sensitivity. Consuming gluten can lead to digestive issues, inflammation, fatigue, and other uncomfortable symptoms. Therefore, avoiding gluten-containing foods is crucial for these individuals to maintain their health and well-being.

Chicken and rice, as a classic comfort food combination, can be a source of solace and satisfaction for many people. However, traditional recipes often include ingredients that contain gluten, such as breadcrumbs or sauces thickened with wheat flour. This presents a challenge for individuals with gluten sensitivities who want to enjoy this comforting dish without compromising their dietary restrictions.

Here is where the significance of gluten-free chicken and rice comfort meals comes into play. By modifying the traditional recipe with gluten-free alternatives, individuals with sensitivities can still indulge in this nostalgic and comforting dish. Gluten-free breadcrumbs or other alternative coatings can be used to achieve the same crispy texture on the chicken, while gluten-free sauces and seasonings can enhance the flavor profile of the dish. Additionally, using naturally gluten-free grains like rice or quinoa instead of wheat-based ingredients ensures that the meal remains safe and enjoyable for those with sensitivities.

The availability of gluten-free products and recipes has significantly improved in recent years, making it easier for individuals with sensitivities to enjoy a wide variety of gluten-free comfort foods. Gluten-free chicken and rice dishes are now commonly found in restaurants and can even be prepared at home with the abundance of gluten-free ingredients available on the market.

The importance of gluten-free chicken and rice comfort meals extends beyond the satisfaction of cravings and nostalgia. It allows individuals with sensitivities to enjoy a familiar and comforting dish, promoting a sense of inclusivity and normalcy. Everyone should have the opportunity to indulge in their favorite comfort foods, and gluten-free options ensure that individuals with sensitivities can also partake in these culinary delights without compromise.

the importance of gluten-free chicken and rice comfort meals for those with sensitivities cannot be overstated. It provides a sense of comfort, satisfaction, and inclusion for individuals who may feel restricted by their dietary restrictions. By modifying traditional recipes and utilizing gluten-free alternatives, individuals with sensitivities can enjoy the same level of comfort and nostalgia as those without dietary restrictions. Gluten-free chicken and rice comfort meals pave the way for a more inclusive and fulfilling dining experience.

Chapter 10. Special Occasions

Valentine's Day Tomato Bisque: Love in Every Spoonful

Valentine's Day is a special occasion celebrated all over the world on February 14th. While many people associate it with romantic love and gifts, Valentine's Day is about much more than that. It is a day to express love, gratitude, and appreciation for those who hold a special place in our lives. One way to convey these emotions is by preparing a delicious meal that brings warmth and comfort to the table. Among the various dishes that can be served on this day, Valentine's Day Tomato Bisque stands out as a perfect representation of love and care.

Tomato bisque is a classic soup made from ripe tomatoes, cream, and a blend of aromatic herbs and spices. Its rich and smooth texture, combined with the vibrant color of the tomatoes, makes it a visually appealing and appetizing dish. But what makes Valentine's Day Tomato Bisque truly special is the effort and love that goes into its preparation.

To begin with, selecting the right tomatoes is crucial. Ripe, juicy tomatoes are not only the key ingredient in the bisque but also symbolize the love and passion that we put into creating a memorable Valentine's Day experience. The tomatoes are carefully hand-picked, ensuring that only the finest ones make it into the soup. This attention to detail reflects the level of care we want to express to our loved ones.

The process of making Valentine's Day Tomato Bisque involves a series of precise and deliberate steps. The tomatoes are first blanched and peeled to ensure a smooth consistency. Then, they are simmered with onions, garlic, and herbs until all the flavors meld together harmoniously. A touch of cream is added to enhance the richness and velvety texture of the bisque.

While the preparation itself requires time and patience, it is an act of love that creates a wonderful sensory experience for both the cook and the recipient. The aroma of simmering tomatoes fills the kitchen, evoking feelings of warmth and comfort. Each step in the process is done with care and intention, resulting in a soup that is not only nourishing but also emotionally satisfying.

The act of serving Valentine's Day Tomato Bisque is equally significant. As the soup is ladled into serving bowls, it is done so with grace and elegance, mirroring the love and appreciation we have for the person we are sharing this meal with. A final touch of garnish, such as a sprinkle of fresh herbs or a drizzle of olive oil, adds a touch of beauty and enhances the overall presentation.

When it comes time to taste the Valentine's Day Tomato Bisque, the flavors burst forth, enveloping the palate in a symphony of taste sensations. The combination of the sweet and tangy tomatoes, the creamy texture, and the harmonious blend of herbs and spices create a divine experience that warms the heart and nourishes the soul.

Valentine's Day Tomato Bisque is not just a soup but a representation of love in every spoonful. Its preparation involves careful selection of ingredients, precise cooking techniques, and a whole lot of heart. By sharing this special dish with our loved ones on Valentine's Day, we express our love, gratitude, and appreciation in a tangible and delicious way. So, whether you are celebrating with a partner, family, or friends, let Valentine's Day Tomato Bisque be a reminder of the love and care we have for those who matter most in our lives.

Easter Ham and Pea Joy: A Springtime Celebration

Easter is a celebration that holds religious and cultural significance for many individuals around the world. Alongside this significance, certain food traditions have emerged, with Easter ham and pea joy being prominent examples. This aims to explore the importance of these delicacies in the context of Easter and springtime celebrations.

Easter ham, traditionally prepared by roasting a whole ham, has become a centerpiece of Easter feasts in many cultures. The ham is often glazed with a sweet and savory mixture, giving it a deliciously caramelized exterior. This succulent meat symbolizes abundance and renewal, reflecting the joyous and thankful spirit of Easter. The act of roasting a ham also brings people together, as family and friends gather around the table to enjoy this festive meal.

In addition to Easter ham, pea joy is another culinary aspect that adds vibrancy and flavor to the festive occasion. Peas are a springtime vegetable that symbolizes fertility, new beginnings, and growth. This humble legume is often cooked and prepared as a side dish, sometimes seasoned with herbs or combined with other ingredients. Alongside the ham, it provides a burst of fresh taste and adds a touch of green to the Easter feast.

The importance of Easter ham and pea joy extends beyond their taste and visual appeal. These dishes carry a deep cultural heritage and serve as reminders of shared traditions and familial connections. For many, the preparation and consumption of these foods are intimate rituals that have been passed down through generations, fostering a sense of continuity and belonging.

Moreover, Easter ham and pea joy exemplify the spirit of gratitude and abundance associated with Easter. The ham, derived from a large animal, represents the bountiful offerings of nature and the generosity of the earth. Meanwhile, peas, a humble crop, remind us to appreciate the simple joys and small blessings that spring brings.

Furthermore, these culinary traditions have the power to unite communities and strengthen social bonds. Easter gatherings provide an opportunity for loved ones to come together, reconnect, and celebrate. Sharing a meal centered on ham and peas creates a space for meaningful conversations, laughter, and the formation of lasting memories.

Easter ham and pea joy play a significant role in the celebration of Easter and the arrival of spring. They not only tantalize our taste buds but also encapsulate the essence of this festive occasion. These culinary traditions bring families and communities together, symbolize abundance and renewal, and embody the spirit of gratitude and appreciation. So, as we savor the succulent ham and the vibrant peas, let us remember the deeper meanings and the joy they bring to Easter and springtime celebrations.

Comforting Chicken and Dumplings: A Taste of Home

Chicken and dumplings is a classic comfort food dish that holds a special place in many people's hearts. This delightful and heartwarming dish brings a sense of nostalgia and invokes fond memories of home-cooked meals with loved ones. The importance of comforting chicken and dumplings goes beyond its delicious taste; it is a symbol of warmth, love, and a connection to our roots.

One of the reasons why chicken and dumplings is so important is its ability to provide comfort during difficult times. Whether you're feeling homesick, stressed, or in need of a pick-me-up, a steaming bowl of chicken and dumplings can instantly soothe your soul. Its hearty and rich flavors, combined with soft and fluffy dumplings, create a soothing sensation that warms you from the inside out. The act of indulging in this comforting dish can transport you back to a simpler time, reminding you of the love and care that went into preparing it.

Chicken and dumplings also serves as a culinary representation of the importance of family and tradition. It is a dish that has been passed down through generations, gathering families together around the dinner table. The process of making chicken and dumplings often involves a shared effort, with multiple family members coming together to chop vegetables, roll out dumplings, and simmer the broth. This communal cooking experience creates a bond and strengthens family ties, making it more than just a meal – it becomes a cherished tradition.

Furthermore, chicken and dumplings is not only a comfort food but a versatile one as well. It can be customized to fit different tastes and dietary preferences. Whether you prefer a creamy broth or a more broth-like consistency, want to add extra vegetables, or even make it gluten-free, chicken and dumplings can be adapted to suit your needs. This adaptability allows individuals to create a dish that brings them comfort and satisfaction, tailored to their personal preferences.

In addition to its emotional significance, chicken and dumplings also carries some health benefits. The chicken provides a good source of lean protein, while the vegetables add essential vitamins and minerals to the dish. Dumplings, although indulgent, can also provide a source of carbohydrates, offering a well-rounded and nourishing meal. This combination of flavors and nutrients makes chicken and dumplings not only a soul-satisfying dish but a nutritionally balanced one too.

comforting chicken and dumplings is more than just a culinary delight – it represents the importance of home, family, and tradition. Its ability to soothe, nourish, and bring people together is what makes it a truly special dish. Whether it's the aroma that fills the kitchen, the memories it evokes, or the feeling of warmth it provides, chicken and dumplings will always hold a special place in our hearts as a taste of home.

Chapter 11.   Worldly Wonders

Mediterranean Chickpea Delight: A Taste of Greece

The Mediterranean Chickpea Delight: A Taste of Greece is a dish that brings together the vibrant flavors of the Mediterranean region. This delightful dish is made with fresh and simple ingredients, showcasing the essence of Greek cuisine.

One of the main reasons why Mediterranean Chickpea Delight is important is its nutritional value. Chickpeas, which form the base of this dish, are rich in protein, fiber, vitamins, and minerals. They are also a great source of plant-based protein, making them an excellent option for vegetarians and vegans. The dish also incorporates a variety of colorful vegetables, such as tomatoes, cucumbers, and bell peppers, which provide essential vitamins and antioxidants.

Another significant aspect of this dish is its cultural significance. Greece is known for its healthy and flavorful cuisine, and this dish embodies the essence of Greek flavors. It is a prime example of the Mediterranean diet, which is recognized worldwide as one of the healthiest diets due to its emphasis on fresh produce, whole grains, and olive oil. By showcasing the flavors and culinary traditions of Greece, Mediterranean Chickpea Delight helps to promote Greek culture and cuisine.

Furthermore, the Mediterranean Chickpea Delight offers a delicious and fulfilling meal option. It can be enjoyed as a main course or as a side dish, making it versatile and adaptable to different dining preferences. The combination of chickpeas, vegetables, and a tangy dressing creates a symphony of flavors that is sure to tantalize the taste buds. Whether served as part of a Greek-inspired feast or enjoyed on its own, Mediterranean Chickpea Delight never fails to satisfy.

the importance of Mediterranean Chickpea Delight: A Taste of Greece lies in its nutritional value, cultural significance, and deliciousness. By incorporating wholesome ingredients and traditional Greek flavors, this dish not only nourishes the body but also celebrates Greek cuisine. So why not indulge in this delightful Mediterranean treat and experience a taste of Greece firsthand?

Thai Red Curry Elegance: A Journey to Southeast Asia

Thai red curry is a dish that represents the perfect blend of flavors, spices, and aromas. It is not just a culinary delight, but also a cultural experience that takes you on a journey to the vibrant and diverse region of Southeast Asia.

One of the key reasons why Thai red curry holds such importance is its unique combination of ingredients. The curry paste, made with red chili peppers, garlic, lemongrass, ginger, and other aromatic herbs and spices, creates a rich and complex flavor profile. The addition of coconut milk brings a creamy and velvety texture that balances out the heat and spice of the curry.

The use of fresh herbs and vegetables further adds to the elegance and vibrancy of the Thai red curry. Thai basil, kaffir lime leaves, and cilantro are commonly used to enhance the freshness of the dish. These ingredients not only provide a burst of flavor but also contribute to the visual appeal with their vibrant colors.

The importance of Thai red curry extends beyond its exquisite taste. It serves as a testament to the cultural heritage and traditions of Southeast Asia. Thailand, in particular, is renowned for its culinary expertise, and Thai red curry shines as one of its signature dishes.

This dish reflects the philosophy of balance that is deeply ingrained in Thai cuisine. The combination of sweet, sour, spicy, and salty flavors creates a harmonious symphony that tantalizes the taste buds. Thai red curry embodies the notion of yin and yang, where contrasting elements come together to create a holistic and well-rounded experience.

Furthermore, Thai red curry is a dish that brings people together. Sharing a steaming bowl of red curry with friends and family is not just about enjoying a meal, but about fostering connections and creating lasting memories. The act of preparing and sharing this dish has been passed down through generations, preserving cultural traditions and strengthening social bonds.

In addition to its cultural significance, Thai red curry also boasts health benefits. The use of fresh ingredients, such as vegetables and herbs, provides a multitude of vitamins, minerals, and antioxidants. The combination of coconut milk and spices like turmeric and ginger may have anti-inflammatory properties and aid digestion.

Overall, Thai red curry represents the elegance of Southeast Asian cuisine. It is a dish that captivates the senses, transports you to distant lands, and nurtures both body and soul. Its importance goes beyond a mere meal, as it symbolizes the richness of culture, traditions, and the art of culinary craftsmanship. Whether enjoyed in Thailand or anywhere else in the world, Thai red curry is a gastronomic experience that embodies the spirit of Southeast Asia.

Swedish Meatball Comfort: Nordic Cuisine at Its Best

Swedish meatballs are more than just a delicious dish - they represent the heart and soul of Nordic cuisine. With their rich history and comforting flavors, Swedish meatballs have become a prominent symbol of Swedish culture and gastronomy.

One of the key reasons why Swedish meatballs hold such importance is their role in bringing people together. In Nordic countries, mealtimes are often seen as a time for family and friends to gather and bond. Swedish meatballs, with their warm and hearty nature, are the perfect dish to accompany these cherished moments. Served with lingonberry sauce, creamy gravy, and buttery mashed potatoes, Swedish meatballs provide comfort and satisfaction to all who indulge in them.

Another aspect that makes Swedish meatballs exceptional is the meticulous attention to detail that goes into their preparation. Traditionally, a mixture of ground beef and ground pork is combined with breadcrumbs, onions, and aromatic spices like nutmeg and allspice. This careful combination of ingredients creates a unique flavor profile that sets Swedish meatballs apart from other meatball variations. Furthermore, their small size allows for a quick and even cooking process, ensuring that they are tender and juicy.

Swedish meatballs also play a significant role in preserving cultural heritage. Passed down through generations, the knowledge and techniques required to make authentic Swedish meatballs are cherished and celebrated. Whether it's a family recipe handed down from grandmother to mother or a treasured secret shared among chefs, Swedish meatballs represent a connection to the past and a way to honor traditions.

Moreover, Swedish meatballs have gained global recognition, becoming one of the most iconic dishes of Nordic cuisine. Thanks to the worldwide success of Swedish furniture giant IKEA, Swedish meatballs have found their way onto plates in various corners of the globe. This popularity has helped Swedish cuisine gain a broader appreciation, showcasing the rich flavors and culinary heritage of the Nordic region.

Swedish meatballs hold immense importance in Nordic cuisine. They not only offer a comforting and delicious dining experience but also serve as a symbol of togetherness, cultural heritage, and the international appeal of Nordic cuisine. Whether enjoyed at home, at a traditional Swedish restaurant, or at an IKEA cafeteria, Swedish meatballs are a true delight that embodies the essence of comfort and Nordic culinary excellence.

Chapter 12. Exotic Escapes

Cuban Black Bean and Plantain Delight: Caribbean Inspiration

Black beans and plantains are integral ingredients in traditional Cuban cuisine. The combination of these two ingredients in a dish called Cuban Black Bean and Plantain Delight creates a unique and flavorful culinary experience. This dish reflects the rich cultural heritage and diverse flavors of the Caribbean region.

Black beans, also known as frijoles negros in Spanish, are a staple in Cuban cooking. They are a great source of protein, fiber, and essential nutrients. Black beans are not only nutritious but also have a creamy texture and earthy taste that enhances the flavor profile of dishes. They are traditionally cooked low and slow with various herbs, spices, and aromatics to create a thick, rich sauce.

Plantains, on the other hand, are a type of starchy fruit that is similar in appearance to bananas. They are used in both savory and sweet dishes throughout the Caribbean. Green plantains are used when they are starchy and firm, while ripe plantains with black skins are used when they are sweet and soft. In this dish, ripe plantains are commonly used to add a subtle sweetness and a soft, melt-in-your-mouth texture.

To prepare Cuban Black Bean and Plantain Delight, black beans are cooked with onion, garlic, bell pepper, and aromatic spices like cumin and oregano. The slow cooking process allows the flavors to meld together, resulting in a deliciously savory black bean sauce. The plantains are usually sliced and caramelized until golden brown, adding a touch of sweetness to balance the flavors.

The combination of black beans and plantains in this dish creates a perfect harmony of flavors. The earthiness of the black beans is complemented by the natural sweetness of the plantains. The contrasting textures of the soft beans and the caramelized plantains add depth to each bite.

Cuban Black Bean and Plantain Delight can be enjoyed as a main dish or as a side dish accompanied by white rice and a variety of other traditional Caribbean side dishes. The dish is often garnished with fresh cilantro or parsley for added freshness and a burst of flavor.

In addition to its delicious taste, this dish holds cultural significance. It represents the fusion of African, Spanish, and Indigenous influences that have shaped Cuban cuisine over centuries. It is a testament to the diverse cultural heritage of the Caribbean region.

Cuban Black Bean and Plantain Delight showcases the importance of these two ingredients in Caribbean cuisine. The combination of black beans and plantains creates a harmonious balance of flavors and textures that is both satisfying and culturally significant. Whether enjoyed as a main dish or as a side, this delightful creation is a true reflection of the vibrant culinary traditions of the Caribbean.

Moroccan Harira Magic: A Trip to North Africa

Moroccan cuisine is renowned for its rich flavors, vibrant spices, and unique dishes. One such dish that stands out is the famous Moroccan Harira soup. This flavorful and hearty soup has become a symbol of Moroccan culture and is enjoyed by locals and tourists alike. We will explore the importance of Moroccan Harira Magic and its significance in North African cuisine.

Moroccan Harira is a traditional soup that is commonly consumed during the holy month of Ramadan. It is enjoyed as a way to break the fast at sunset and is packed with nutritious ingredients that provide sustenance after a day of fasting. The soup is made from a base of tomatoes, lentils, chickpeas, and various spices such as cinnamon, ginger, and turmeric. The addition of meat, usually lamb or chicken, adds depth and richness to the soup.

One of the key reasons why Moroccan Harira is so important in North African cuisine is its ability to bring people together. In Moroccan culture, food is often seen as a way to connect with others and share experiences. During Ramadan, families and communities gather to share the Iftar meal, which often includes a bowl of Harira. This communal aspect of enjoying a warm bowl of soup creates a sense of unity and togetherness.

Beyond its cultural significance, Moroccan Harira is also known for its nutritional value. The soup is packed with protein, fiber, and essential vitamins and minerals. Lentils and chickpeas provide a good source of plant-based protein, while tomatoes offer a dose of vitamin C and antioxidants. The addition of spices not only enhances the flavor but also brings numerous health benefits. Ginger, for example, aids digestion and reduces inflammation, while turmeric has powerful antioxidant properties.

Furthermore, the preparation of Moroccan Harira is an art form in itself. Each family and region in Morocco may have their own unique twist on the recipe, resulting in a wide variety of flavors and techniques. The process of making Harira involves slow cooking the ingredients, allowing the flavors to meld together and create a harmonious blend. The use of traditional cooking methods, such as simmering over a low flame, further adds to the enchanting magic of this dish.

Moroccan Harira Magic holds great importance in North African cuisine. Its cultural significance, ability to bring people together, and its nutritional value make it a beloved dish in Moroccan households. From its rich flavors to its heartwarming qualities, Moroccan Harira is more than just a soup - it is a symbol of traditions, community, and the magic of Moroccan cuisine.

Filipino Kare-Kare Comfort: Exploring Southeast Asian Flavors

Filipino Kare-Kare is a traditional dish that holds significant importance in Filipino cuisine. Its rich and flavorful taste, coupled with its cultural and historical background, makes it a staple comfort food for Filipinos.

Kare-Kare is a savory stew made primarily with oxtail or tripe, accompanied by various vegetables such as eggplant, bok choy, and string beans. The dish is known for its distinct orange color, which comes from the annatto seeds used in its preparation. The creamy and thick peanut sauce is what sets Kare-Kare apart from other stews, giving it a unique taste and texture.

One can trace the roots of Kare-Kare to the pre-colonial era of the Philippines. It is believed to have originated from the indigenous Tagalogs and Kapampangans, who used peanuts as a key ingredient in their cuisine. Over time, Kare-Kare evolved and incorporates Spanish and Chinese influences, making it a true fusion dish.

The popularity of Kare-Kare extends beyond the borders of the Philippines. It has gained recognition in the international culinary scene, drawing food enthusiasts and travelers from all around the world. The dish showcases the complexity and diversity of Southeast Asian flavors, reflecting the region's vibrant culinary heritage.

What makes Kare-Kare even more significant is its role in Filipino culture and history. It is often served during special occasions and gatherings, symbolizing unity and togetherness. In Filipino households, preparing Kare-Kare is seen as a labor of love, as it requires time and effort to create its distinctive flavors.

The importance of Filipino Kare-Kare goes beyond being just a comforting and delicious dish. It represents the Filipino spirit, resilience, and the ability to adapt and embrace different influences. Through its unique blend of flavors and cultural significance, Kare-Kare showcases the rich tapestry of Filipino cuisine and serves as a bridge to indulge in the diverse food heritage of Southeast Asia.

Chapter 13. Family Favorites

Irish Potato and Leek Classic: A Taste of Ireland

Irish Potato and Leek Classic: A Taste of Ireland is a dish that reflects the history and traditions of Ireland. This flavorful and hearty stew is strongly tied to Ireland's rural, agrarian past. In the olden days, a family's wealth was measured by how many pigs and acres of potatoes they owned.

This will dive into the ingredients, the varying components of the dish, its place in Irish culture, and its importance in Ireland's history.

Ingredients:

Irish Potato and Leek Classic is made with simple, yet flavorful ingredients. The foundation of this dish is, of course, potatoes. Potatoes have been cultivated in Ireland for hundreds of years. Growing well in Ireland's mild, moist climate, this vegetable quickly became a staple.

Leeks also play a pivotal role in the dish. The allium is indigenous to central and northern Europe, and have been a part of Irish cuisine since they were introduced to the region.

Modern renditions of this traditional dish may also include ingredients like carrots, onions, garlic, and cream.

Wholesome Ingredients and Nutritional Value:

The dish is a nutritious and filling meal. Potatoes are packed with carbohydrates, vitamin C, vitamin B6, magnesium, and iron.

It is a good source of dietary fiber, supporting digestive health, maintaining blood sugar and cholesterol levels.

Leeks are high in folic acid, which helps the body make new cells and is especially important during pregnancy. It is rich in many vitamins (A, B, and C) and minerals, particularly manganese and iron.

The inclusion of cream adds richness to the stew. However, the dish can also be prepared without it.

Hungarian Mushroom Magic: A Culinary Adventure in Eastern Europe

Hungarian Mushroom Magic: A Culinary Adventure in Eastern Europe is an exceptional gastronomic experience that showcases the rich culture and heritage of Hungary. This will delve into the importance of this unique culinary adventure and shed light on its significance in Eastern Europe.

Hungarian cuisine is renowned for its bold flavors and use of fresh, natural ingredients. The introduction of Hungarian Mushroom Magic has elevated the culinary landscape of Eastern Europe by adding a new dimension to traditional dishes. This culinary adventure focuses on the intricate preparation and enchanting flavors of mushroom-based recipes, showcasing the versatility of this ingredient.

One of the key reasons why Hungarian Mushroom Magic is important in Eastern Europe is its role in preserving traditional Hungarian cuisine. By highlighting mushroom-based recipes, this culinary adventure ensures that these traditional dishes are not forgotten or overshadowed by modern trends. This helps in maintaining the culinary legacy of Hungary and passing it on to future generations.

Moreover, Hungarian Mushroom Magic promotes environmentally friendly practices by encouraging the use of locally sourced mushrooms. This not only supports local farmers but also reduces the carbon footprint associated with transportation. It emphasizes the importance of sustainable food production and showcases how small changes in ingredient sourcing can make a big impact.

Another aspect that makes Hungarian Mushroom Magic significant in Eastern Europe is its cultural significance. Food has always been intertwined with culture, and this culinary adventure acts as a gateway to explore Hungarian traditions, stories, and history. By incorporating these elements into the experience, participants gain a deeper understanding of Hungary's rich heritage.

Additionally, Hungarian Mushroom Magic contributes to the tourism industry by attracting food enthusiasts and travelers from all over the world. The unique experience offered by this culinary adventure sets Hungary apart from other destinations in Eastern Europe. It enhances the country's reputation as a culinary hotspot and creates opportunities for local businesses and communities to thrive.

Hungarian Mushroom Magic: A Culinary Adventure in Eastern Europe plays a crucial role in preserving traditional Hungarian cuisine, promoting sustainability, showcasing cultural heritage, and boosting the tourism industry. Through its unique focus on mushroom-based recipes, this culinary adventure enhances the gastronomic landscape of Eastern Europe, capturing the hearts and taste buds of food enthusiasts worldwide.

Dutch Split Pea and Ham Joy: Dutch Delicacy

Dutch Split Pea and Ham Joy, also known as Erwtensoep or Snert, is a traditional Dutch dish that holds great importance in Dutch cuisine. This hearty soup is especially popular during the winter months, as it provides warmth and comfort to those who indulge in its delicious flavors.

One of the main ingredients in Dutch Split Pea and Ham Joy is, as the name suggests, split peas. These peas are dried and then split in half, resulting in a smooth and creamy texture when cooked. Split peas are known for their nutritional benefits, as they are a good source of fiber, protein, and various vitamins and minerals.

Another essential component of this dish is the ham, which adds a rich and savory taste. The ham is typically smoked and diced before being added to the soup, providing a depth of flavor that complements the split peas perfectly. The combination of the earthy taste of the split peas and the smoky goodness of the ham creates a harmonious balance that delights the taste buds.

To make Dutch Split Pea and Ham Joy, the split peas are first soaked overnight to soften them. Then, a medley of vegetables such as onions, carrots, and leeks are sautéed to enhance the soup's flavor. The split peas and ham are added to the pot, along with water or broth, and the soup is left to simmer for several hours. As it cooks, the flavors meld together, resulting in a thick and hearty soup that is as comforting as it is tasty.

This traditional Dutch delicacy is not only beloved for its deliciousness but also for its cultural significance. Dutch Split Pea and Ham Joy is often enjoyed as a special treat during festive occasions, such as New Year's Day, and is considered a symbol of good luck and prosperity for the coming year.

Furthermore, the simplicity of the ingredients used in this dish reflects the resourcefulness of the Dutch people. Split peas and ham were readily available and affordable, making this soup a staple in Dutch households for centuries. It embodies the Dutch philosophy of making the most out of humble ingredients by transforming them into something extraordinary.

Dutch Split Pea and Ham Joy is a cherished Dutch delicacy that holds both gastronomic and cultural significance. Its wholesome ingredients, comforting flavors, and historical importance make it a true gem of Dutch cuisine. So, the next time you have a chance to savor this hearty soup, embrace the Dutch culinary tradition and experience the joy of Dutch Split Pea and Ham Joy.

Chapter 14. Culinary Adventures

Vietnamese Pho Noodle Wonder: The Art of Pho

Pho, a traditional Vietnamese noodle soup, is not just a culinary delight, but also an exquisite art form on its own. Vietnamese Pho Noodle Wonder: The Art of Pho encapsulates the essence and significance of this beloved dish in Vietnamese culture.

The importance of Pho lies in its ability to bring people together, nourish the body, and showcase the rich heritage of Vietnam. As a staple dish that can be found on almost every street corner in Vietnam,

Pho serves as a symbol of unity and bonding. Families and friends gather around steaming bowls of Pho, sharing stories and creating lasting memories. It is a communal experience that celebrates the traditions and values of Vietnamese society.

Beyond its social significance, Pho is a culinary masterpiece that requires skill, craftsmanship, and attention to detail. The art of Pho lies not only in its complex flavors but also in the meticulous preparation and presentation. The broth, simmered for hours with a blend of fragrant spices, takes on a depth of flavor that is both comforting and soul-soothing. The noodles, made from rice or wheat, are cooked to perfection, creating a satisfyingly chewy texture. The dish is then elevated with an assortment of toppings, such as thinly sliced beef or chicken, fresh herbs, bean sprouts, and lime wedges.

Pho is also a representation of Vietnam's rich cultural heritage. The dish is believed to have originated in the North of Vietnam during the early 20th century and has since become a national treasure. It reflects the fusion of various culinary influences, including Chinese and French, showcasing Vietnam's history and international connections. The art of Pho has been passed down through generations, with each family adding their own unique touch to the recipe. It is a living testament to the country's resilience and ability to adapt and innovate.

Moreover, the popularity of Pho has transcended borders and gained international recognition. It has become a global phenomenon, loved by people from all walks of life. The art of Pho has successfully introduced Vietnamese culture to the world, becoming an ambassador of Vietnamese cuisine. Its delicacy and complexity have captivated the taste buds of many, making it a sought-after dish in restaurants around the globe.

Vietnamese Pho Noodle Wonder: The Art of Pho is more than just a dish. It is a cultural treasure that brings people together, showcases culinary expertise, and represents Vietnam's rich history and international connections. The art of Pho is an intricate masterpiece that continues to enchant and inspire, making it an essential part of Vietnamese identity.

Peruvian Chicken and Quinoa Euphoria: A Taste of the Andes

The importance of Peruvian Chicken and Quinoa Euphoria: A Taste of the Andes lies in its rich history, cultural significance, and health benefits. Peruvian Chicken, also known as Pollo a la Brasa, is a traditional Peruvian dish that has gained popularity worldwide. Its roots can be traced back to the Inca Empire, where it was commonly consumed for its nutritional value and delicious flavor.

One of the main reasons Peruvian Chicken is highly regarded is its unique cooking method. The chicken is marinated in a blend of spices, including cumin, garlic, and paprika, then cooked rotisserie-style over charcoal. This cooking technique infuses the meat with smoky flavors and results in a juicy and tender texture that is hard to replicate.

Another aspect that contributes to the importance of Peruvian Chicken is its cultural significance. In Peru, this dish holds a special place in the hearts of the locals. It is often enjoyed during family gatherings, festivals, and celebrations. The preparation and serving of Peruvian Chicken have become iconic, showcasing the country's culinary heritage and traditions.

Additionally, Peruvian Chicken has gained global recognition for its health benefits. It is a lean source of protein, which makes it a great choice for individuals looking to maintain a balanced diet. The marinade used in the cooking process also adds depth of flavor without adding excessive calories or unhealthy fats.

Alongside Peruvian Chicken, Quinoa Euphoria: A Taste of the Andes complements the dish perfectly. Quinoa is a grain-like seed that originated in the Andean region thousands of years ago. It was a staple food for the Incas and has recently gained recognition as a superfood due to its numerous health benefits.

Quinoa is packed with essential nutrients, including fiber, iron, and magnesium. It is gluten-free and has a complete protein profile, containing all nine essential amino acids. This makes it an excellent choice for vegetarians and vegans who are looking for a plant-based protein source.

Furthermore, Quinoa Euphoria adds an element of excitement and variety to the overall dining experience. The dish combines quinoa with vibrant ingredients such as roasted vegetables, avocado, and tangy lime dressing. The result is a refreshing and wholesome salad that perfectly complements the flavors of Peruvian Chicken.

Peruvian Chicken and Quinoa Euphoria: A Taste of the Andes are not only delicious culinary creations but also hold great importance. They showcase the cultural heritage of Peru, offer a healthy and nutritious dining option, and bring people together to celebrate and enjoy the flavors of the Andean region.

Indonesian Soto Ayam Adventure: A Flavorful Journey to Indonesia

Indonesian cuisine is known for its rich flavors and diverse ingredients, and one dish that perfectly embodies these qualities is Soto Ayam. Soto Ayam is a traditional chicken soup that is enjoyed throughout Indonesia and holds a special place in the country's culinary heritage.

One of the reasons why Indonesian Soto Ayam is important is because it reflects the country's cultural and culinary diversity. Indonesia is a vast archipelago with over 17,000 islands, and each region has its own unique flavors and cooking styles. Soto Ayam is a dish that can be found in various regions of Indonesia, but with slight variations in ingredients and preparation methods. This reflects the diversity of Indonesia's culinary traditions and brings people together through their shared love for this dish.

Another importance of Indonesian Soto Ayam is its role in preserving traditional cooking methods and ancestral recipes. Many Indonesians learned how to cook Soto Ayam from their parents or grandparents, and it has been passed down through generations. By continuing to make and enjoy Soto Ayam, Indonesians can keep their culinary heritage alive and maintain a connection to their roots.

Furthermore, Indonesian Soto Ayam Adventure offers a unique opportunity for food enthusiasts to explore the diverse flavors and ingredients of Indonesian cuisine. From tender chicken pieces simmered in aromatic broth to the fragrant blend of herbs and spices, Soto Ayam offers a truly immersive culinary experience. It allows travelers to not only indulge in the delicious flavors but also learn about the local ingredients, cooking techniques, and cultural significance of this beloved dish.

Additionally, the popularity of Indonesian Soto Ayam has contributed to the growth of culinary tourism in Indonesia. Many tourists visit Indonesia specifically to explore the country's rich food culture, and Soto Ayam is often at the top of their must-try list. This has led to the establishment of Soto Ayam-focused food tours, cooking classes, and restaurants, creating new job opportunities and promoting economic growth in the tourism sector.

Indonesian Soto Ayam Adventure: A Flavorful Journey to Indonesia is of great importance for several reasons. It showcases the cultural diversity of Indonesia, preserves traditional cooking methods, offers a unique culinary experience, and contributes to the growth of culinary tourism. Through Soto Ayam,

Indonesians and visitors alike can appreciate the rich flavors and heritage of Indonesian cuisine and embark on a flavorful journey that will leave a lasting impression.

Chapter 15. Soup for the Soul

Ukrainian Borscht Beet Bliss: From Eastern Europe with Love

Borscht, a traditional Ukrainian beet soup, holds a special place in the hearts and palates of many Eastern Europeans. Its vibrant colors, rich flavors, and nutritional benefits make it a popular dish that has been enjoyed for centuries. This will explore the importance of Ukrainian Borscht and its enduring legacy.

First and foremost, Ukrainian Borscht is a symbol of cultural heritage and identity. Originating in Ukraine, this hearty soup has been passed down through generations, becoming a beloved tradition in Eastern European households. Its preparation involves a careful selection of seasonal vegetables, particularly beets, which give it its distinctive ruby-red hue. Borscht is often considered a national dish of Ukraine, representing the country's rich culinary heritage.

Aside from its cultural significance, Ukrainian Borscht also offers numerous health benefits. The main ingredient, beets, are known for their high nutritional value. They contain essential vitamins and minerals, including vitamin C, iron, and potassium. Additionally, beets are a rich source of antioxidants, which are beneficial for overall health and wellbeing. When combined with other vegetables and herbs such as cabbage, carrots, and dill, Borscht becomes a wholesome and nourishing meal.

Furthermore, Ukrainian Borscht stands out for its versatility. While the traditional recipe includes beets, cabbage, potatoes, and meat, variations of Borscht can be found throughout Eastern Europe. Some regions substitute the base ingredients with more local produce, such as tomatoes or mushrooms, creating unique flavor profiles. Borscht can also be adjusted to vegetarian or vegan preferences by omitting the meat and using vegetable broth. This adaptability allows individuals from diverse backgrounds to enjoy Borscht while still preserving its essence.

In addition to its cultural and health aspects, Borscht plays a significant role in fostering community and social connections. The preparation of Borscht often involves multiple family members or friends, creating a cooperative and inclusive atmosphere. It is not uncommon to see several generations come together to chop vegetables, simmer the soup, and share stories, passing down traditions and strengthening bonds. Borscht is frequently served during special occasions, holidays, and community gatherings, making it a symbol of togetherness and celebration.

Ukrainian Borscht is more than just a soup. It represents the cultural heritage of Eastern Europe, offering a glimpse into traditional cooking practices and customs. Its nutritional benefits, adaptability, and ability to bring people together make it an essential part of the culinary world. Whether enjoyed in a small family setting or a large community gathering, Ukrainian Borscht continues to be cherished, spreading the love and joy it was born from.

Jewish Matzo Ball Splendor: A Delicate Delight

Jewish Matzo Ball Splendor is a culinary delight that holds great significance in Jewish cuisine. Matzo balls, also known as knaidlach, are fluffy and tender dumplings made from matzo meal, eggs, and a few other key ingredients. Although seemingly simple, the art of making perfect matzo balls requires skill and precision.

The importance of Jewish Matzo Ball Splendor goes beyond its delicious taste. It is a dish that brings people together, symbolizing the unity and bond of Jewish communities. Matzo balls are commonly served during special occasions such as Passover Seders, weddings, and festive gatherings. They are a staple in Jewish comfort food and hold a special place in the hearts of many.

The delicate texture of matzo balls adds a unique element to Jewish cuisine. Whether served in a flavorful chicken soup or as a standalone dish, matzo balls are a cherished part of Jewish culinary heritage. They offer a satisfying and comforting experience, reminiscent of home-cooked meals passed down through generations.

Furthermore, Jewish Matzo Ball Splendor represents the resilience and adaptability of the Jewish people. Matzo, the key ingredient in matzo balls, holds deep symbolism in Jewish culture. It is unleavened bread, symbolizing the haste in which the Israelites had to leave Egypt during the Exodus. Matzo balls carry this history and act as a reminder of the perseverance and strength of the Jewish community.

Jewish Matzo Ball Splendor is more than just a delightful culinary creation. It is a dish that embodies the unity, tradition, and resilience of Jewish culture. Its delicate texture and rich history make it a cherished delicacy among Jewish communities worldwide. Whether enjoyed during special occasions or as a comforting meal, Jewish Matzo Ball Splendor continues to bring joy and connection to those who indulge in its delicacy.

Finnish Salmon Soup Elegance: A Nordic Treat

The importance of Finnish Salmon Soup Elegance cannot be overstated. As a traditional dish in Nordic cuisine, it embodies the rich culinary heritage and cultural significance of Finland.

Finnish Salmon Soup is a delicious delicacy that combines the freshest ingredients with meticulous cooking techniques. The key to its elegance lies in the harmonious balance of flavors and textures.

The star ingredient, fresh salmon, is carefully selected for its quality and taste. The tender and succulent salmon pieces are cooked to perfection, allowing their natural flavors to shine through.

Complementing the salmon are a variety of vegetables such as potatoes, carrots, and leeks. These vegetables add depth and complexity to the soup while maintaining a refreshing and light quality.

To achieve true elegance, Finnish Salmon Soup is traditionally seasoned with dill, a quintessential herb in Nordic cuisine. The aromatic and slightly tangy flavor of dill enhances the overall taste profile of the soup, creating a truly delightful experience for the senses.

Beyond its culinary merits, Finnish Salmon Soup holds a special place in Finnish culture. It is often enjoyed during festive occasions and family gatherings, symbolizing unity and togetherness. The act of sharing this dish fosters a sense of community and connection among individuals.

Furthermore, Finnish Salmon Soup Elegance represents the sustainable and responsible nature of Nordic cuisine. The ingredients used in this dish are sourced locally and seasonally, minimizing the carbon footprint and supporting local communities.

Finnish Salmon Soup Elegance is not just a culinary delight, but a symbol of Finnish heritage and values. Its flavor, freshness, and cultural significance make it an exceptional Nordic treat that should be cherished and celebrated.

RECIPES

1) Classic Chicken Noodle Soup

A comforting blend of tender chicken, veggies, and noodles in a savory broth.

Prep time; Ten minutes

Cook Time; Thirty minutes

Serves; 4

Ingredients:

- One tbsp. of olive oil
- One diced onion
- Two cloves of minced garlic
- Two carrots, sliced
- Two celery stalks, sliced
- Four cups chicken broth
- Two cups cooked chicken, shredded
- One cup egg noodles
- One bay leaf
- Salt & pepper, as required
- Chopped fresh parsley for garnish

Directions:

1. In a large pot over medium heat, warm the olive oil. Add the garlic and onion, and cook until aromatic and transparent.

2. When the celery and carrots start to soften, cook them for about 5 minutes after adding them to the pot.

3. For about 10 minutes, reduce the heat to low and simmer after adding the chicken broth and bringing it to a boil.

4. Put the bay leaf in the skillet with the cooked chicken and egg noodles. Keep the noodles cooking for another 10 to 15 minutes, or until they reach the desired tenderness.

5. To taste, add salt and pepper.

6. Remove the bay leaf before serving.

7. Garnish with chopped fresh parsley.

Nutrition: Calories: 250 Fat: 8g Carbs: 25g Protein: 18g

A rich and aromatic tomato soup infused with fresh basil.

Prep time; Ten minutes

Cook Time; Thirty minutes

Serves; 4

Ingredients:

- Two tbsp. olive oil
- One chopped of onion
- Three cloves of minced garlic
- Four cups fresh tomatoes, chopped
- One cup tomato sauce
- One cup vegetable broth
- One tbsp. balsamic vinegar
- One tbsp. sugar
- One-fourth cup fresh basil leaves, chopped
- Salt & pepper, as required

Directions:

1. Olive oil should be heated over medium heat in a big saucepan.

2. After dicing the onion and garlic, place the ingredients in the saucepan and set the heat to medium. Saute for five minutes, or until the onion is translucent and the garlic has developed its characteristic aroma.

3. Cook the freshly chopped tomatoes in the pot for a further five minutes, or until they begin to soften.

4. Add the sugar, fresh basil leaves, balsamic vinegar, tomato sauce, and vegetable broth.

5. Season to taste with salt and pepper.

6. Cook the soup with the lid on for 20 minutes at a low heat.

7. smooth up the soup by blending it or with an immersion blender.

8. Return the soup to the saucepan and simmer for another five minutes.

9. To serve, sprinkle with additional fresh basil leaves and heat through.

Nutrition: Calories: 180 Fat: 8g Carbs: 25g Protein: 4g

NOTES:

_____

_____

_____

A satisfying Italian soup with a medley of vegetables and pasta.

Prep time; Fifteen minutes

Cook Time; Forty-five minutes

Serves; 4

Ingredients:

- Two tbsp. olive oil
- One chopped of onion
- Two carrots, diced
- Two celery stalks, diced
- Three cloves of minced garlic
- One zucchini, diced
- One yellow squash, diced
- One can of diced tomatoes (14.5 ounces)
- Four cups vegetable broth
- Two cups water
- One cup small pasta (such as elbow or ditalini)
- One can (15 ounces) of rinsed and drained kidney beans
- Fresh green beans, trimmed and sliced into 1-inch pieces, one cup
- One cup of fresh or frozen corn kernels
- One tsp. of dried basil
- One tsp. of dried oregano
- Salt & pepper, as required
- Parmesan cheese, grated, for serving.
- For garnish, use fresh basil leaves

Directions:

1. Olive oil must be heated over medium heat in a large saucepan. The onions, garlic, celery, and carrots should be added now. Saute the vegetables for about 5 minutes, or until tender.

2. Cook the yellow squash and zucchini in the pot for a further 3 minutes.

3. Add the water, vegetable broth, and diced tomatoes. Heat till boiling.

4. Include the pasta, dried oregano, dry basil, dried green beans, kidney beans, corn, and salt and pepper. Mix thoroughly.

5. After the pasta has cooked for 15 to 20 minutes, or turn the heat down to a simmer and cook until the vegetables are cooked.

6. If necessary, taste and adjust the seasonings.

7. Garnish with freshly chopped basil leaves and grated Parmesan cheese and a steaming serving.

Nutrition: Calories: 320 Fat: 8g Carbs: 52g Protein: 14g

NOTES:

_____

_____

_____

A zesty soup featuring lentils, sausage, and a kick of spice.

Prep time; Fifteen minutes

Cook Time; Forty-five minutes

Serves; 4

Ingredients:

- One cup dried lentils
- One tbsp. of olive oil
- One chopped of onion
- Two cloves of minced garlic
- Two diced carrots
- Two celery stalks, diced
- Eight ounces spicy sausage, sliced
- One tsp. paprika
- One-half tsp. cayenne pepper
- One tsp. cumin
- Four cups chicken broth
- One can diced tomatoes
- Salt & pepper, as required
- Fresh parsley, for garnish (optional)

Directions:

1. Rinse the dried lentils and set aside.

2. Olive oil should be heated in a large pot set over medium heat. Put in the vegetables, onion, garlic, and celery. The vegetables should be cooked for around 5 minutes.

3. Cook the sausage pieces in the pot for 7 to 8 minutes, or until they are browned.

4. Add the cumin, cayenne, and paprika and stir. Simmer for 1 or 2more minutes.

5. Put in the lentils, chicken stock, and diced tomatoes. Reduce heat to a simmer and cook for 30−35 minutes, or until lentils are mushy, after bringing to a boil.

6. Add salt & pepper to taste as needed.

7. If wanted, top hot dish with fresh parsley.

Nutrition: Calories: 350 Fat: 12g Carbs: 30g Protein: 24g

A silky miso broth with tofu and seaweed, a Japanese favorite.

Prep time; Ten minutes

Cook Time; Twenty minutes

Serves; 4

Ingredients:

- Four cups vegetable broth
- Three tbsp. white miso paste
- One cup firm tofu, cubed
- One cup sliced mushrooms
- Two green onions, thinly sliced
- Two tbsp. soy sauce
- One tbsp. sesame oil
- One tsp. grated ginger
- Two cloves of minced garlic
- One tbsp. rice vinegar
- One tbsp. mirin (optional)
- One tsp. sugar (optional)
- Fresh cilantro, for garnish
- Sesame seeds, for garnish

Directions:

1. In a large enough pot, bring the vegetable broth to a boil.

2. Whisk together the miso paste and a tablespoon of the hot broth in a small bowl.

3. Put in the pot the miso paste, the tofu, the mushrooms, the green onions, the soy sauce, the sesame oil, the grated ginger, and the minced garlic. Mix by stirring.

4. To let the flavors melt together, reduce the heat to medium-low and simmer for ten to fifteen minutes.

5. Add the sugar (if using), rice vinegar, and mirin. If necessary, adjust the seasonings by tasting them.

6. Spoon soup into dishes; top with sesame seeds and fresh cilantro.

Nutrition: Calories: 180 Fat: 9g Carbs: 13g Protein: 15g

NOTES:

_____
_____
_____

A nutritious soup with roasted veggies and protein-packed quinoa.

Prep time; Fifteen minutes

Cook Time; Forty minutes

Serves; 4

Ingredients:

- One cup of quinoa
- Two cups of vegetable broth
- One medium diced of onion
- Two cloves of minced garlic
- Two carrots, peeled and chopped
- Two celery stalks, chopped
- One bell pepper, diced
- One zucchini, diced
- One cup butternut squash, diced
- Two tbsp. of olive oil
- One tsp. of dried thyme
- One tsp. of dried oregano
- One-half tsp. of paprika
- Four cups of vegetable broth
- Salt & pepper, as required

Directions:

1. Preheat the oven to 400 degrees Fahrenheit (around 200 degrees Celsius).

2. Arrange the bell pepper, zucchini, butternut squash, carrots, and celery in chopped form on a baking sheet. Add a drizzle of olive oil and season with salt, pepper, paprika, dried oregano, and dried thyme. Make sure all the vegetables are coated with the seasonings by tossing everything together.

3. Roast the vegetables for 20 to 25 minutes in a preheated oven, or until they are soft and gently browned.

4. The minced garlic and diced onion are sautéed in olive oil until fragrant and the onion is translucent in a big pot.

5. To get rid of any bitterness, rinse the quinoa under cold water. Stir the quinoa occasionally while cooking it for one to two minutes in the pot.

6. Add the veggie broth and heat until it boils. Once the quinoa is cooked and has absorbed the liquid, turn the heat down to low, cover the saucepan, and let the food simmer for 15 to 20 minutes.

7. Remove the roasted vegetables from the oven and add them to the pot with the cooked quinoa and broth. Stir well to combine.

8. Add pepper and salt to flavor prior to serving. Allow the mixture to percolate for an additional 5 minutes so the flavors can combine.

9. Present the hot Quinoa and Roasted Vegetable Soup and relish!

Nutrition: Calories: 250 Fat: 8g Carbs: 38g Protein: 9g

NOTES:

_____
_____
_____

A healthy green soup with tender white beans.

Prep time; Fifteen minutes

Cook Time; Twenty minutes

Serves; 4

Ingredients:

- One tbsp. olive oil
- One small onion, diced
- Two cloves of minced garlic
- One can white beans, rinsed and drained
- One bunch spinach, washed and chopped
- One tsp. of dried oregano
- One-half tsp. of salt
- One-fourth tsp. of black pepper
- One-fourth tsp. of red pepper flakes (optional)
- One-half cup vegetable broth
- One lemon, juiced
- Parmesan cheese, grated (optional)

Directions:

1. In a large skillet, preheat the olive oil over medium heat. Cook the onion and garlic in a skillet for two to three minutes, or until aromatic and translucent.

2. Fill the skillet with the white beans, spinach, salt, red pepper, and black pepper flakes (if using). Toss to thoroughly mix in all the ingredients.

3. Fill the skillet with the veggie stock and cook it. Simmer for approximately five minutes, or until the flavors meld and the spinach wilts.

4. Take the skillet off of the burner and pour one lemon's juice over the mixture. Make sure to thoroughly mix in the lemon juice.

5. As a side dish or over cooked rice or pasta, serve the hot Spinach and White Bean Delight. If preferred, Parmesan cheese gratings are sprinkled on top.

Nutrition (per serving): Calories: 180 Fat: 4g Carbs: 28g Protein: 10g

NOTES:

_____

_____

_____

A velvety soup made from roasted butternut squash, perfect for fall.

Prep time; Twenty minutes

Cook Time; Forty-five minutes

Serves; 4

Ingredients:

- One butternut squash (about 2 pounds)
- Two tbsp. of olive oil
- One tsp. salt
- One-half tsp. of black pepper
- One-half tsp. of dried thyme
- One-fourth cup of grated Parmesan cheese
- One-fourth cup of chopped fresh parsley

Directions:

1. Preheat oven to 425 degrees Fahrenheit (220 degrees C). Prepare a parchment paper-lined baking sheet before beginning.

2. Cut the butternut squash into 1-inch cubes after peeling and seeding it.

3. Combine the olive oil, salt, pepper, and dried thyme with the butternut squash cubes in a big basin and toss until thoroughly coated.

4. Arrange the coated squash cubes on the baking sheet that has been preheated in a single layer.

5. Roast, tossing once halfway through cooking, at 400 degrees for 40 to 45 minutes, or until the squash is tender and begins to caramelize, if using a preheated oven.

6. Take out the roasted butternut squash and place it on a platter for presentation.

7. Sprinkle freshly minced parsley and grated Parmesan cheese over the roasted squash.

8. Gently toss to mix.

9. Serve warm.

Nutrition (per serving): Calories: 180 Fat: 8g Carbs: 28g Protein: 3g

NOTES:

_____

_____

_____

A vibrant soup bursting with the goodness of carrots and anti-inflammatory turmeric.

Prep time; Fifteen minutes

Cook Time; Twenty-five minutes

Serves; 4

Ingredients:

- Four large carrots, peeled and sliced
- One tbsp. of turmeric powder
- One tsp. of cumin powder
- One tsp. of coriander powder
- One tsp. paprika
- One tbsp. olive oil
- Salt & pepper, as required
- Chopped fresh coriander leaves for garnish

Directions:

1. Combine the sliced carrots, olive oil, salt, pepper, cumin, coriander, and turmeric powder in a big bowl. Mix everything until the carrots are coated all over.

2. Turn the oven on to 400°F, or 200°C.

3. In a single layer on a baking sheet, place the seasoned carrots.

4. Carrots need to be roasted for 25 minutes in a preheated oven to become tender and caramelized.

5. Take them out of the oven and give them some time to cool.

6. Place the roasted carrots in a serving bowl and top with the chopped cilantro.

7. Enjoy while it's still hot!

Nutrition: Calories: 80 Fat: 4g Carbs: 10g Protein: 1g

NOTES:

_____

_____

_____

A hearty soup packed with kale, chickpeas, and a boost of nutrients.

Prep time; Fifteen minutes

Cook Time; Twenty-five minutes

Serves; 4

Ingredients:

- One tbsp. of olive oil
- One diced of onion
- Three cloves of minced garlic
- Four cups vegetable broth
- Two cups chopped kale leaves
- One can (Fifteen oz) chickpeas, rinsed and drained
- One can (14.5 oz) of diced tomatoes
- One tsp. of dried thyme
- One tsp. of dried oregano
- Salt & pepper, as required

Directions:

1. The olive oil should be warmed up in a big pot over medium heat. Cook the onion and garlic together until the onions are translucent.

2. Add the veggie broth and heat until it boils.

3. Include the diced tomatoes, dried oregano, dried thyme, and chopped kale leaves. To taste, season with salt and pepper.

4. Cook the kale for 20 minutes over low heat, or until tender.

5. Serve the hot soup and savor it!

Nutrition: Calories: 198 Fat: 4g Carbs: 32g Protein: 10g

NOTES:

_____

_____

_____

A classic combo of broccoli and cheddar in a creamy base.

Prep time; Fifteen minutes

Cook Time; Thirty minutes

Serves; 4

Ingredients:

- Two cups broccoli florets
- Two tbsp. butter
- One small onion, diced
- Two cloves of minced garlic
- Three tbsp. of all-purpose flour
- Two of cups milk
- Two cups chicken or vegetable broth
- Two cups shredded cheddar cheese
- Salt & pepper, as required

Directions:

1. The broccoli florets should be blanched in simmering water for two to three minutes, or until just tender. Remove and lay aside the contents.

2. Melt the butter in the same kettle over low to medium heat. Add the minced garlic and onion, and cook for an additional 5 minutes, or until the garlic and onion are soft.

3. Dredge the garlic and onions in the flour, then well mix to coat. To eliminate the taste of raw flour, heat for one to two minutes.

4. Stirring constantly while slowly whisking in the milk and broth will help prevent lumps from forming. The sauce can be thickened by simmering it for about 5 minutes at a low heat.

5. Turn the heat down to low and toss in the shredded cheddar cheese until it melts and becomes smooth.

6. Return the blanched broccoli florets to the pot and stir so that the cheesy sauce coats them. For complete heating, cook for a further 2-3 minutes.

7. Season with Salt & pepper, as required.

8. Serve the Creamy Broccoli Cheddar Bliss hot, garnished with additional shredded cheddar cheese if desired.

Nutrition: Calories: 325 Fat: 20g Carbs: 15g Protein: 20g

A traditional Italian soup with pasta and beans in a flavorful broth.

Prep time; Ten minutes

Cook Time; Thirty minutes

Serves; 4

Ingredients:

- One tbsp. of olive oil
- One medium diced onion
- Two cloves of minced garlic
- Two celery stalks, diced
- Two carrots, diced
- One can (14 oz) diced tomatoes
- Four cups vegetable broth
- One can (14 oz) cannellini beans, rinsed and drained
- One cup of small pasta (such as elbow macaroni or ditalini)
- One tsp. of dried oregano
- One tsp. of dried basil
- Salt & pepper, as required
- Chopped fresh parsley (as a garnish)

Directions:

1. Olive oil should be heated in a large pot set over medium heat. Carrots, celery, onions, and garlic should be sautéed for about 5 minutes, or until soft.

2. Put the tomato sauce, broth, beans, herbs (basil, oregano, and salt and pepper), and cannellini in a pot. Once everything is mixed and boiling, turn the heat down to a simmer for 15 minutes.

3. In the meantime, prepare the pasta as directed on the package, cooking it until it's al dente. Empty and place aside.

4. Add the cooked pasta to the soup pot after it has simmered for fifteen minutes. Mix thoroughly to blend.

5. Simmer the soup for a further 5 minutes to give the flavors time to combine.

6. Garnish with freshly cut parsley and serve hot.

Nutrition: Calories: 300 Fat: 5g Carbs: 55g Protein: 10g

A sweet and savory soup with the goodness of sweet potatoes and apples.

Prep time; Fifteen minutes

Cook Time; Forty-five minutes

Serves; 4

Ingredients:

- Two cubed and peeled medium sweet potatoes
- Two apples, peeled, cored, and diced
- One-fourth cup of brown sugar
- One-fourth cup of melted butter
- One-half tsp. of cinnamon
- One-fourth tsp. of nutmeg
- One-fourth tsp. of salt
- One-fourth cup of chopped pecans

Directions:

1. Set oven temperature to 190°C/375°F.

2. Put the apples, sweet potatoes, brown sugar, melted butter, nutmeg, cinnamon, and salt in a big basin. To coat all the ingredients, thoroughly mix.

3. Put the mixture into an oiled baking dish.

4. Sprinkle the chopped pecans over the top.

5. Cover the dish with foil and bake it for 30 minutes.

6. Take off the foil and bake for a further fifteen minutes, or until the top is golden brown and the sweet potatoes are soft.

7. Wait a few minutes for it to cool down after you take it out of the oven.

Nutrition: Calories: 280 Fat: 12g Carbs: 42g Protein: 3g

NOTES:

_____
_____
_____

A childhood favorite in soup form, complete with mac 'n' cheese.

Prep time; Ten minutes

Cook Time; Twenty-five minutes

Serves; 4

Ingredients:

- Eight ounces elbow macaroni
- Two tbsp. unsalted butter
- One small onion, diced
- Two cloves of minced garlic
- Two tbsp. all-purpose flour
- Two cups vegetable broth
- One cup milk
- One (14.5-ounce) can crushed tomatoes
- One cup shredded cheddar cheese
- One-fourth cup grated Parmesan cheese
- One-half tsp. of dried basil
- One-half tsp. of dried oregano
- One-half tsp. salt
- One-fourth tsp. of black pepper
- One-fourth tsp. of red pepper flakes (optional)
- Chopped fresh basil, for garnish

Directions:

1. Prepare the elbow macaroni per the directions on the package. Empty and place aside.

2. In a large saucepan, melt the butter over low to medium heat. The onion and garlic should be simmered for about 5 minutes, or until they are soft.

3. To cook the flour, sprinkle it over the onions and garlic and stir constantly for 1-2 minutes.

4. Add the milk and vegetable broth gradually and whisk until smooth. Simmer the mixture for a while.

5. Add the dried oregano, dried basil, dried Parmesan cheese, tomatoes crushed with salt, pepper, and optional red pepper flakes. Keep it at a low boil for 10 minutes, stirring occasionally, or until the soup is thoroughly cooked and the cheese has melted.

6. Include the cooked macaroni in the broth and mix everything together. Allow it cook for 5 more minutes to allow flavors to mingle.

7. Present the warm, creamy tomato mac 'n' cheese soup with freshly chopped basil on top.

Nutrition: Calories: 410 Fat: 20g Carbs: 42g Protein: 18g

A velvety soup with potatoes and leeks, a French-inspired delight.

Prep time; Twenty minutes

Cook Time; Thirty minutes

Serves; 4

Ingredients:

- Four medium-sized potatoes, peeled and diced
- Two leeks, sliced
- Two tbsp. butter
- Two cloves of minced garlic
- Two cups of vegetable broth or chicken broth
- One cup of heavy cream
- Salt & pepper, as required

Directions:

1. Butter should be melted in a large pot set over medium heat. Add the garlic and leeks after they have softened, and continue cooking.

2. Fill the pot with the liquid and diced potatoes. Once the potatoes have come to a boil, reduce the heat and let them simmer for about 20 minutes, or until they are tender.

3. Blend or use an immersion blender to process the mixture until it is smooth.

4. Add the heavy cream and stir after returning the combined mixture to the stove. Add salt and pepper to taste as needed.

5. Cook for another 5-10 minutes until heated through.

6. Serve hot and garnish with additional sliced leeks, if desired.

Nutrition: Calories: 325 Fat: 20g Carbs: 30g Protein: 5g

NOTES:

_____

_____

_____

A wallet-friendly soup filled with beans, pasta, and flavor.

Prep time; Ten minutes

Cook Time; Thirty minutes

Serves; 4

Ingredients:

- One tbsp. olive oil
- One medium onion, diced
- Two cloves of minced garlic
- Two carrots, sliced
- Two celery stalks, sliced
- One can of diced (14 ounces) tomatoes
- Four cups of vegetable broth
- One can (Fifteen ounces) kidney beans, rinsed and drained
- One can (Fifteen ounces) cannellini beans, rinsed and drained
- One cup small pasta (such as elbows or shells)
- One tsp. of dried basil
- One tsp. of dried oregano
- Salt & pepper, as required

Directions:

1. Olive oil should be heated in a large saucepan over moderate heat. After around 5 minutes, the onion and garlic should be fragrant and soft.

2. Cook the celery and carrots in the pot for a further five minutes.

3. Put in the diced tomatoes and vegetable broth. Turn the heat down to a simmer once the mixture has come to a boil.

4. Fill the saucepan with the kidney beans, cannellini beans, pasta, dried oregano, and basil. Mix well to blend.

5. Once the pasta and vegetables are soft, cover the saucepan and simmer for 15 to 20 minutes.

6. You can season to taste with salt and pepper.

7. Present heated and savor!

Nutrition (per serving): Calories: 250 Fat: 4g Carbs: 46g Protein: 11g

A simple yet satisfying soup with rice and a mix of veggies.

Prep time; Fifteen minutes

Cook Time; Twenty-five minutes

Serves; 4

Ingredients:

- One cup of rice
- Two cups of vegetable broth
- One tbsp. of olive oil
- One chopped of onion
- Two cloves of garlic, minced
- One bell pepper, diced
- One zucchini, diced
- One cup of corn kernels
- One cup of peas
- One tsp. of cumin
- Salt & pepper, as required

Directions:

1. Bring the vegetable broth to a boil in a pot. When the rice is cooked, add it, cover, and simmer for 15 minutes.

2. Olive oil should be heated in a large skillet over medium heat. Put in the onions and garlic, and sauté until the onions are translucent.

3. Fill the skillet with the bell pepper, zucchini, peas, and corn kernels. Simmer the veggies for 5 minutes, or until they are crisp-tender.

4. Stir in the cooked rice, cumin, salt, and pepper. Toss to combine everything evenly.

5. To give the flavors time to mingle, cook for a further 2 minutes.

Nutrition: Calories: 240 Fat: 4g Carbs: 47g Protein: 6g

NOTES:

_____

_____

_____

A spicy soup featuring tortilla strips, avocado, and Mexican spices.

Prep time; Ten minutes

Cook Time; Twenty minutes

Serves; 4

Ingredients:

- Eight tortillas
- Two tbsp. of olive oil
- One diced of onion
- Two cloves of minced garlic
- One diced of red bell pepper
- One green bell peppers, diced
- One diced and seeded jalapenos
- One tsp. of ground cumin
- One tsp. chili powder
- One-half tsp. salt
- One-fourth tsp. black pepper
- One can (Fifteen ounces) black beans, rinsed and drained
- One cup of corn kernels
- One cup shredded Mexican cheese blend
- Fresh cilantro, for garnish
- Servings of sour cream
- Salsa, for serving

Directions:

1. Olive oil should be heated over medium heat in a large skillet. Put in the garlic, onion, green pepper, and jalapeno. Put the vegetables in water and simmer for 5 minutes, or until they are soft.

2. Put the chili powder, cumin, salt, and pepper into the pan. The ingredients will be more harmonious if you mix them well.

3. Include the corn and black beans in the skillet. Cook for a another three minutes, stirring now and then.

4. Turn the oven on to 375°F, or 190°C.

5. Arrange a tortilla on a sheet pan. Spoon half of the tortilla with the bean and veggie mixture. Add some cheese shreds on top. Gently push the tortilla in half to make it fold.

6. Continue with the remaining tortillas, cheese, and the mixture of beans and vegetables.

7. Bake the filled tortillas for 10 minutes in a preheated oven, or until the tortillas are crispy and the cheese has melted.

8. Cut each tortilla in half or quarters when it has cooled for a few minutes after being removed from the oven.

9. Serve the Mexican tortilla fiesta with fresh cilantro, sour cream, and salsa. Enjoy!

Nutrition (per serving): Calories: 350 Fat: 12g Carbs: 48g Protein: 12g

NOTES:

_____

_____

_____

A soothing Chinese soup with silky egg ribbons in a clear broth.

Prep time; Ten minutes

Cook Time; Fifteen minutes

Serves; 2

Ingredients:

- Two eggs
- Two slices of bread
- Two tbsp. butter
- Salt to taste
- Pepper to taste

Directions:

1. Beat the eggs in a medium-sized basin until thoroughly combined. Add pepper and salt as needed.

2. Melt one tablespoon of butter in a nonstick skillet that is heated to medium heat.

3. Thoroughly coat both sides of each piece of bread by dipping it into the beaten eggs.

4. After dipping the bread pieces, place them in the skillet and cook them for two to three minutes on each side, or until they are golden brown.

5. Take out of the skillet and place the bread slices coated in eggs aside.

6. In the same saucepan, heat the remaining tablespoon of butter.

7. Break the remaining eggs into the skillet and cook, stirring occasionally, until the yolks are still somewhat runny but the whites are set.

8. Cover the bread slices with egg by placing each fried egg on top of them.

9. If needed, add more salt and pepper for seasoning.

10. Serve the Simple Egg Drop Comfort immediately.

Nutrition Information (per serving): Calories: 320 Fat: 20g Carbs: 20g Protein: 14g

NOTES:

_____

_____

_____

A hearty beef stew with tender meat and vegetables.

Prep time; Twenty minutes

Cook Time; Three hours

Serves; 6

Ingredients:

- Two lbs beef stew meat, cubed
- One-fourth cup all-purpose flour
- Two tbsp. olive oil
- One chopped of onion
- Three cloves of minced garlic
- Four carrots, peeled and chopped
- Three potatoes, peeled and cubed
- Two cups beef broth
- One cup red wine
- One can diced tomatoes
- Two bay leaves
- One tbsp. Worcestershire sauce
- Salt & pepper, as required

Directions:

1. Evenly coat the beef stew meat in flour by tossing it in a bowl.

2. Olive oil should be warmed in a big pot over medium heat. When the beef stew meat is coated, add it and heat it until it browns all over. Take out of the pot and place aside.

3. Place the minced garlic and chopped onion in the same pot. When the onion is fragrant and translucent, remove it from the pan.

4. The pot should already have the garlic and onion in it, so add the potatoes and carrots and stir to combine.

5. Add the red wine and beef broth, scraping up any browned bits from the pot's bottom.

6. Include the chopped tomatoes, Worcestershire sauce, bay leaves, and salt and pepper to taste.

7. Put the browned beef stew meat back in the pot and heat it up to a boiling point. When it reaches a boil, reduce the heat and cover the pot. Stir occasionally and simmer for two to three hours.

8. If wanted, top the hot beef stew with chopped parsley. Have fun!

Nutrition: Calories: 400 Fat: 15g Carbs: 25g Protein: 35g

A flavorful Thai soup with coconut milk and aromatic spices.

Prep time; Fifteen minutes

Cook Time; Thirty minutes

Serves; 4

Ingredients:

- Two tbsp. of vegetable oil
- One onion, sliced
- Two cloves of minced garlic
- One sliced of red bell pepper
- One sliced of green bell pepper
- One thinly sliced of carrot
- One can (400ml) coconut milk
- Two tbsp. Thai red curry paste
- Two tbsp. soy sauce
- One tbsp. brown sugar
- One tbsp. lime juice
- One cup broccoli florets
- One cup sliced mushrooms
- One cup snap peas
- One cup diced tofu or chicken (optional)
- Fresh basil leaves, for garnish
- Ready-to-serve cooked rice

Directions:

1. In a large pan or wok, heat the vegetable oil over moderate heat.

2. When the onion and garlic are aromatic, add them to the skillet and sauté for two to three minutes.

3. Include the snap peas, carrot, broccoli, mushrooms, red and green bell peppers, and tofu or chicken (if using). Cook, stirring periodically, for 5 minutes.

4. In a small bowl, mix the Thai red curry paste, coconut milk, lime juice, soy sauce, brown sugar, and brown sugar. Stir the ingredients together after adding them to the pan.

5. After the vegetables are cooked to your preference, reduce the heat to low and simmer for 15 to 20 minutes.

6. Sprinkle some fresh basil leaves over hot rice and then top with Thai coconut curry.

Nutrition: Calories: 350 Fat: 20g Carbs: 30g Protein: 10g

A creamy soup showcasing tender clams and potatoes.

Prep time; Fifteen minutes

Cook Time; Forty minutes

Serves; 4

Ingredients:

- Two pounds fresh clams
- Four slices bacon, diced
- One chopped of onion
- Two celery stalks, chopped
- Two cloves of minced garlic
- Three potatoes, peeled and cubed
- Two cups clam juice
- One cup chicken broth
- One cup heavy cream
- Two tbsp. all-purpose flour
- Salt & pepper, as required
- Fresh parsley (chopped) (as a garnish)

Directions:

1. Scrub the clams under cold water to remove any dirt or grit. Discard any clams that are open or broken.

2. Cook the bacon in a big pot over medium heat until it's crispy. Using a slotted spoon, remove the bacon and reserve for garnish.

3. Add the chopped celery, onion, and garlic to the same saucepan. Cook for about 5 minutes, or until the vegetables are tender.

4. Add the diced potatoes, chicken broth, and clam juice to the pot. Turn the heat down to a simmer once the mixture has come to a boil. The potatoes should be cooked for around 15 minutes in a simmering water bath.

5. Take the clams out of their shells and cut them into smaller pieces while the potatoes are cooking.

6. In a separate small skillet over medium heat, melt the butter. Mixing with flour creates a roux.

Cook for one to two minutes, or until the mixture starts to become brown.

7. Add the heavy cream gradually, whisking to ensure no lumps form. Cook and whisk the mixture until it thickens.

8. Add the cream mixture to the pot along with the stock and potatoes. Add the chopped clams and stir.

9. When you've reached the desired seasoning, add salt and pepper to taste and continue simmering for 5 more minutes to let the flavors meld.

10. Top the hot chowder with fresh parsley and the crispy bacon that was set aside.

Nutrition: Calories: 350 Fat: 22g Carbs: 25g Protein: 16g

NOTES:

_____

_____

_____

A classic French onion soup with caramelized onions and melted cheese.

Prep time; Twenty minutes

Cook Time; One hour

Serves; 4

Ingredients:

- Four large onions
- Four tbsp. of butter
- Two tsp. of sugar
- Two tbsp. of flour
- Four cups of beef broth
- One cup of white wine
- One bay leaf
- Salt and pepper, to taste
- Four pieces of bread, crusty
- One and one-half cups of grated Gruyere cheese

Directions:

1. Slice the onions thinly.

2. In a large saucepan, melt the butter over low to medium heat. Sliced onions should be added and cooked for 30 minutes, rotating occasionally, until caramelized.

3. After the onions have caramelized, sprinkle them with sugar and simmer for a further five minutes.

4. Stir continuously for one minute after adding the flour to the pot.

5. Add the white wine and beef broth gradually while stirring. Add the bay leaf and season with salt and pepper.

6. Cook the mixture for 30 minutes, bringing it to a simmer.

7. While the soup is simmering, toast the slices of crusty bread until crispy.

8. Preheat the broiler.

9. Take out the bay leaf from the soup and pour it into bowls that are safe to bake.

10. Top each bowl of soup with a toasted bread piece and a little shredded Gruyere cheese.

11. If you want bubbling, melted cheese, broil the bowls for two to three minutes.

12. Serve heated and savor! 9. Take out the bay leaf from the soup and pour it into bowls that are safe to bake.

10. Top each bowl of soup with a toasted bread piece and a little shredded Gruyere cheese.

11. Broil the bowls for two to three minutes, or until the cheese is bubbling and melted.

12. Serve heated and savor!

Nutrition: Calories: 400 Fat: 20g Carbs: 40g Protein: 14g

NOTES:

_____

_____

_____

The foundation for countless soup creations, a homemade chicken stock.

Prep time; Ten minutes

Cook Time; Three hours

Serves; 8

Ingredients:

- One whole chicken, about four pounds
- Two large onions, peeled and quartered
- Four carrots, peeled and chopped
- Four celery stalks, chopped
- Four garlic cloves, smashed
- Two bay leaves
- One tbsp. whole black peppercorns
- Two tsp. salt
- Eight cups water

Directions:

1. Add the chicken, onions, celery, garlic, peppercorns, carrots, bay leaves, and salt to a large stockpot.

2. Put in some water and get it boiling over medium heat.

3. Put the lid on the pan and reduce the heat to low. Simmer for three hours, skimming off any foam that rises to the surface.

4. Take the chicken out of the saucepan and let it to cool. After the chicken has cooled down, take out the flesh and set it aside for later use.

5. Transfer the stock to a big container by straining it through a fine-mesh sieve. Throw away the solids.

6. Once the stock has cooled completely, you may keep it in the fridge for up to 5 days or freeze it for up to 3 months.

Nutrition: Calories: 50 Fat: 2g Carbs: 1g Protein: 7g

NOTES:

_____

_____

_____

A meatless chili filled with beans, veggies, and bold flavors.

Prep time; Twenty minutes

Cook Time; One hour

Serves; 8

Ingredients:

- Two tbsp. olive oil
- One large onion, diced
- Three cloves of minced garlic
- Two bell peppers, diced
- Two carrots, diced
- One zucchini, diced
- Two cans (14 ounces each) of diced tomatoes
- Two cans (14 ounces each) of kidney beans, rinsed and drained
- One can (14 ounces) black beans, rinsed and drained
- One can of drained (14 ounces) corn
- Two tbsp. of chili powder
- One tsp. of cumin
- One tsp. of paprika
- Salt & pepper, as required

Directions:

1. Olive oil should be warmed in a big pot over medium heat. When the onion is translucent and tender, add the garlic and onion.

2. Cook the carrots, zucchini, and bell peppers in the saucepan for a further 5 minutes, or until the veggies begin to soften.

3. Add the corn, kidney beans, black beans, and diced tomatoes and stir. Add the paprika, cumin, chili powder, salt, and pepper. Blend thoroughly.

4. Simmer the chili for a short while before turning down the heat. Cook, covered, stirring periodically, for 45 minutes to 1 hour.

5. Taste and, if necessary, adjust the seasoning.

6. Top the hot vegetarian chili with your preferred toppings, including chopped cilantro, sour cream, or shredded cheese.

Nutrition: Calories: 250 Fat: 6g Carbs: 40g Protein: 11g

A robust soup featuring beef, barley, and a savory broth.

Prep time; Fifteen minutes

Cook Time; Two hours

Serves; 4

Ingredients:

- One lb beef stew meat, cubed
- One onion, diced
- Two carrots, sliced
- Two celery stalks, chopped
- Three cloves of minced garlic
- One cup pearl barley
- Four cups beef broth
- One bay leaf
- Salt & pepper, as required

Directions:

1. Heat some oil in a big pot over medium heat. Once added, sauté the beef until browned.

2. Put all the vegetables in the pot: garlic, onion, celery, and carrots. Soften the vegetables in a sauté pan.

3. Add the salt, pepper, bay leaf, barley, and beef broth. Once the barley is cooked and the beef is soft, reduce heat and simmer for 1.5 to 2 hrs.

4. Before serving, take out the bay leaf. If necessary, taste and adjust the seasoning.

Nutrition: Calories: 400 Fat: 10g Carbs: 45g Protein: 30g

NOTES:

_____

_____

_____

A smoky and savory black bean soup, perfect with a dollop of sour cream.

Prep time; Ten minutes

Cook Time; Twenty-five minutes

Serves; 4

Ingredients:

- One tbsp. olive oil
- One small diced onion
- Two cloves of minced garlic
- One diced red bell pepper
- One jalapeno pepper, diced and seeded (optional)
- One tsp. ground cumin
- One tsp. smoked paprika
- One-half tsp. chili powder
- One-half tsp. salt, or to taste
- Two cans (Fifteen ounces each) black beans, rinsed and drained
- One can diced (14.5 ounces) tomatoes
- One cup vegetable broth
- One tbsp. lime juice
- Fresh cilantro, chopped, for garnish

Directions:

1. Olive oil should be heated at a medium temperature in a big pot. To soften the onion, add it to the simmering mixture and let it sit for about 5 minutes.

2. Cook for 2 more minutes after adding the garlic, red bell pepper, and jalapeo pepper (if using).

3. Spice it up by mixing in some salt, chili powder, smoked paprika, and ground cumin. For one minute, toast the spices.

4. Include the vegetable broth, sliced tomatoes, and black beans. After bringing to a simmer, cook for 15 to 20 minutes, or until the flavors are well combined.

5. Olive oil should be heated over moderate heat in a big saucepan. Sauté the onion for about 5 minutes, or until it has softened.

6. Cook for 2 more minutes after adding the garlic, red bell pepper, and jalapeo (if using).

7. Mix in the smoked paprika, smoked chili powder, chili powder, and ground cumin. Toast the spices for a minute in a hot pan.

8 Put in some black beans, tomato dices, and veggie stock. Slowly boil for 15–20 minutes to allow flavors to combine.

9. Add lime juice and stir.

10. Serve the smoky black bean wonder hot, garnished with fresh cilantro.

Nutrition: Calories: 250 Fat: 5g Carbs: 42g Protein: 12g

NOTES:

_____

_____

_____

A Tex-Mex favorite with tender chicken, tortilla strips, and spices.

Prep time; Fifteen minutes

Cook Time; Twenty-five minutes

Serves; 4

Ingredients:

- One tbsp. of olive oil
- One diced of onion
- Two cloves of minced garlic
- One diced of red bell pepper
- One diced of green bell pepper
- One jalapeno pepper, diced and seeded
- One tsp. of ground cumin
- One tsp. of chili powder
- One tsp. of paprika
- One-half tsp. of salt
- One-fourth tsp. of black pepper
- Two cups cooked chicken, shredded
- One cup frozen corn kernels
- One can diced (14 ounces) tomatoes
- One can of (Eight ounces) tomato sauce
- One cup chicken broth
- Eight small flour tortillas
- One cup shredded cheddar cheese
- Garnishing with finely minced fresh coriander

Directions:

1. To begin, heat the olive oil in a large skillet over medium heat. Vegetables such as onions, green peppers, red peppers, and jalapenos can be added. Fork-tender vegetables require roughly 5 minutes of simmering at a low heat.

2. Ground cumin, paprika, chili powder, salt, and pepper should all be added to the pan. Toss the vegetables so that the seasonings are well distributed.

3. Fill the pan with the cooked chicken, tomato sauce, frozen corn kernels, diced tomatoes, and chicken broth. Mix thoroughly to blend. To enable the flavors to merge, bring the mixture to a simmer and cook for ten minutes.

4. Turn the oven on to 375°F, or 190°C.

5. Fill the center of each flour tortilla with a tiny bit of the chicken mixture. The tortillas should be rolled up and put seam-side down in a baking dish.

6. Top the rolled tortillas with the cheddar cheese that has been shredded.

7. To melt the cheese and make it bubbly, bake in a preheated oven for 15 minutes.

8. Before serving, garnish with freshly cut cilantro.

Nutrition: Calories: 420 Fat: 15g Carbs: 45g Protein: 25g

NOTES:

_____

_____

_____

A timeless split pea soup, thick and hearty.

Prep time; Fifteen minutes

Cook Time; One hour and thirty minutes

Serves; 6

Ingredients:

- Two cups dried split peas
- One large chopped of onion
- Two cloves of minced garlic
- Two carrots, diced
- Two celery stalks, diced
- One bay leaf
- Four cups vegetable broth
- Four cups water
- Salt & pepper, as required

Directions:

1. Olive oil should be heated in a large pot set over medium heat. Combine the vegetables, onion, garlic, and celery. Put the vegetables in water and simmer for 5 minutes, or until they are soft.

2. Pour water, vegetable broth, dried split peas, and a bay leaf into the pot. Turn down the heat and simmer the peas for an hour, or until tender, after bringing to a boil.

3. After removing the bay leaf, purée the soup until it's smooth using an immersion blender or a standard blender. Alternatively, if you'd like, leave some texture.

4. To taste, season with salt and pepper. Reheat the food.

Nutrition Information: Calories: 250 Fat: 2g Carbs: 46g Protein: 17g

NOTES:

_____

_____

_____

A fragrant lentil soup with Indian spices like cumin and coriander.

Prep time; Ten minutes

Cook Time; Thirty minutes

Serves; 4

Ingredients:

- One cup of red lentils
- Two cups water
- One tbsp. of vegetable oil
- One finely chopped of onion
- Two garlic cloves of minced
- One tsp. grated ginger
- One tsp. of cumin seeds
- One tsp. of ground coriander
- One-half tsp. of turmeric powder
- One-half tsp. of chili powder (adjust to taste)
- One diced of tomato
- One-half cup coconut milk
- Salt to taste
- Chopped fresh coriander leaves for garnish

Directions:

1. Thoroughly rinse and drain the lentils.

2. Put the lentils in a big pot and cover them with water, then bring to a boil. Lentils take about 15–20 minutes to become soft during cooking. Take out the surplus water.

3. Vegetable oil should be heated in a separate pan over moderate heat. After adding the cumin seeds, let them a moment to crackle.

4. Include and sauté the onion until it is translucent.

5. Include the grated ginger and minced garlic. Add another minute of sautéing.

6. Include the chili powder, turmeric powder, and ground coriander. Once combined, heat for 1 minute.

7. Include the chopped tomato and heat it until it gets tender.

8. Stir thoroughly to mix the cooked lentils with the spices in the pan.

9. Add the coconut milk, then mix once more. Simmer it for 5 to 10 minutes.

10. Add salt to taste to season.

11. Garnish with fresh cilantro and serve hot.

Nutrition (per serving): Calories: 250 Fat: 8g Carbs: 35g Protein: 12g

NOTES:

_____

_____

_____

A spicy and sour Thai hot pot with shrimp and mushrooms.

Prep time; Fifteen minutes

Cook Time; Twenty minutes

Serves; 4

Ingredients:

- Four cups of water
- Two stalks of lemongrass, bruised
- Four kaffir lime leaves
- Eight slices of galangal
- Two Thai chilies, chopped
- 200g shrimp, peeled and deveined
- 200g chicken breast, sliced
- 200g button mushrooms, sliced
- 200g cherry tomatoes
- 100g baby corn, halved
- Two tbsp. of fish sauce
- Two tbsp. of lime juice
- One tbsp. of soy sauce
- One tbsp. of sugar
- Fresh cilantro leaves, for garnishing

Directions:

1. Boil the water in a big pot.

2. Incorporate Thai chiles, galangal, kaffir lime leaves, and lemongrass into the boiling water. To infuse the flavors, boil it for 5 minutes.

3. Fill the saucepan with the shrimp, chicken, cherry tomatoes, mushrooms, and baby corn. Cook until the beef is thoroughly cooked, about 10 minutes.

4. Add sugar, soy sauce, lime juice, and fish sauce. Tailor the seasonings to your personal preference.

5. Take off the heat and add some fresh cilantro leaves as a garnish.

6. Serve hot alongside steaming rice or rice noodles.

Nutrition Information (per serving): Calories: 250 Fat: 4g Carbs: 20g Protein: 30g

A Mexican soup with hominy corn and your choice of meat.

Prep time; Thirty minutes

Cook Time; Three hours

Serves; 6 servings

Ingredients:

- Two lbs pork shoulder, cut into chunks
- One medium onion, diced
- Three cloves of minced garlic
- Two cans (15 oz each) hominy, drained and rinsed
- Four cups chicken broth
- Two dried ancho chilies, seeded and soaked in hot water
- Two dried guajillo chilies, seeded and soaked in hot water
- One tsp. of dried oregano
- One tsp.of ground cumin
- Salt & pepper, as required

Directions:

1. Place the pork shoulder, chopped onion, minced garlic, and enough water to cover the pork in a big pot. After bringing to a boil, lower heat so that it simmers. Cook until the meat is cooked, about 1 hour.

2. Take the dehydrated chilies out of the hot water and put them in a blender while the pork cooks. If necessary, add a small amount of the chili soaking liquid and blend until smooth.

3. After the pork has cooked for an hour, add the blended chili mixture, hominy, chicken broth, dried oregano, ground cumin, and Salt & pepper, as required. Mix thoroughly to blend.

4. Return the saucepan to a simmer and cook, stirring regularly, for a further 2 hours.

5. After the cooking time is up, taste the pozole and adjust seasonings if necessary.

6. Serve the authentic Mexican pozole hot in bowls, garnished with your choice of toppings such as shredded cabbage, diced chopped of onion cilantro, sliced radishes, and a squeeze of fresh lime juice.

Nutrition:

Per serving: Calories: 400 Fat: 20g Carbs: 25g Protein: 30g

NOTES:

_____
_____
_____

A festive Italian soup with meatballs and greens.

Prep time; Thirty minutes

Cook Time; One hour

Serves; 6-8 servings

Ingredients:

- One pound ground of beef
- One pound ground of pork
- One-half cup of breadcrumbs
- One-fourth cup of Parmesan cheese grated
- Two cloves of minced garlic
- One-fourth cup of chopped fresh parsley
- One-fourth cup of chopped fresh basil
- One-half tsp. salt
- One-fourth tsp. pepper
- Two large eggs, beaten
- Four cups chicken broth
- One cup acini di pepe pasta
- Two cups baby spinach
- One-fourth cup grated Parmesan cheese (for garnish)

Directions:

1. In a large bowl, mix together the ground beef, ground pork, breadcrumbs, grated Parmesan cheese, minced cloves of garlic, chopped parsley, chopped basil, salt, pepper, and beaten eggs. Combine thoroughly so that nothing is left out.

2. Combine the breadcrumbs, ground beef, and ground pork in a sizable bowl.

3.Prepare a big pan by heating it over low to medium heat. When the onion is translucent, add the meatballs and cook for another 5 minutes, turning occasionally. Put the meatballs on a platter and remove them from the pan.

4. Add chicken broth to the same pan and heat to a boil. When the pasta is approximately 10 minutes from being done, add the acini di pepe and stir to combine.

5. The meatballs should be cooked through after being simmered for an additional 10 minutes.

6. When the baby spinach is wilted, add it and continue stirring for an additional two minutes.

7. Serve the Italian Wedding Celebration soup hot, garnished with grated Parmesan cheese.

Nutrition: Each serving contains approximately: Calories: 450 Fat: 20g Carbs: 30g Protein: 35g

A chilled tomato-based soup with a hint of garlic and peppers.

Prep time; Fifteen minutes

Cook Time; No Cooking Time Required

Serves; 4

Ingredients:

- Six ripe tomatoes
- One cucumber
- One red bell pepper
- One small red onion
- Two cloves of garlic
- Two tbsp. of extra-virgin olive oil
- Two tbsp. of red wine vinegar
- Salt & pepper, as required
- One-fourth tsp. cayenne pepper (optional)
- Fresh basil or parsley for garnish

Directions:

1. Finely chop the red onion, bell pepper, cucumber, and tomatoes.

2. Blend or puree the vegetables in a food processor or blender.

3. Put the garlic, olive oil, and red wine vinegar into the blender.

4. If preferred, add cayenne pepper, salt, and pepper for seasoning.

5. Process the mixture until it's smooth and thoroughly mixed.

6. To enable the flavors to mingle, transfer the gazpacho to a big dish or pitcher and place it in the refrigerator for at least an hour.

7. Serve chilled, garnished with fresh basil or parsley.

Nutrition: Calories: 98 Fat: 6g Carbs: 11g Protein: 2g

NOTES:

_____

_____

_____

A creamy and indulgent soup featuring succulent lobster.

Prep time; Twenty minutes

Cook Time; Fifty minutes

Serves; 4

Ingredients:

- Two pounds lobster meat, cooked and chopped
- Four cups lobster stock
- One cup heavy cream
- One-half cup dry white wine
- One chopped of onion
- Two celery stalks, chopped
- Two carrots, chopped
- Four cloves of minced garlic
- Two tbsp. tomato paste
- One bay leaf
- One tsp. paprika
- One-half tsp. dried thyme
- One-fourth tsp. cayenne pepper
- Salt and pepper, to taste
- Two tbsp. of butter
- Freshly chopped parsley as a garnish

Directions:

1. Butter should be melted in a large pot over low to medium heat. Carrots, celery, onions, and garlic should be added as aromatics. To soften the vegetables, put them in a pot of water and simmer for 5 minutes

2. Add the cayenne pepper, dry thyme, paprika, and tomato paste. Add 2 more minutes of cooking.

3. Include the white wine, bay leaf, and lobster stock. After bringing to a simmer, cook for 20 minutes so that the flavors may combine.

4. Remove the bay leaf and use an immersion blender to smooth up the soup. Alternatively, you might use a blender to purée the ingredients.

5. Put the soup back on the stove and add the heavy cream. To taste, season with salt and pepper.

6. When the lobster is well heated, add the chopped lobster meat to the soup and simmer for an additional five minutes.

7. Garnish the hot lobster soup with finely chopped fresh parsley.

Nutrition (per serving): Calories: 450 Fat: 30g Carbs: 15g Protein: 35g

A velvety soup highlighting the delicate flavor of asparagus.

Prep time; Fifteen minutes

Cook Time; Twenty minutes

Serves; 4

Ingredients:

- One-pound asparagus, thinly sliced into pieces measuring one inch
- Two tbsp. butter
- One small chopped of onion
- Two cloves of minced garlic
- Four cups of vegetable broth
- One cup of heavy cream
- Salt & pepper, as required

Directions:

1. Butter should be melted in a large pot over low to medium heat. Simmer for 5 minutes on low heat after adding the onion and garlic.

2. Cook the asparagus in the pot for an additional five minutes, stirring now and then.

3. Put in the vegetable broth and bring to a boil. The asparagus should be simmered over low heat for about 10 minutes, or until tender.

4. Use a blender or an immersion blender to puree the soup until it is smooth.

5. Pour the heavy cream into the soup and return it to the boil. Add salt and pepper to taste as needed.

6. Cook for a further 5 minutes on low heat, or until well cooked.

7. Serve hot and enjoy!

Nutrition: Calories: 250 Fat: 20g Carbs: 12g Protein: 5g

NOTES:

_____
_____
_____

Prep time; Fifteen minutes

Cook Time; Thirty minutes

Serves; 4

Ingredients:

- One pound wild mushrooms, such as chanterelles, porcini, and oyster mushrooms
- Two tbsp. olive oil
- Two cloves of minced garlic
- One shallot, minced
- One tbsp. of fresh thyme leaves
- One tbsp. of fresh parsley, chopped
- Salt & pepper, as required
- One tbsp. butter
- One-fourth cup white wine
- One-fourth cup heavy cream

Directions:

1. After cleaning, chop the mushrooms into small pieces.

2. Warm the olive oil over medium heat in a large skillet. 2-3minutes, or until the shallot, garlic, thyme, and parsley are aromatic.

3. After 8-10 minutes, turn the mushrooms over and continue simmering until they have released their moisture and begun to brown.

4. You can season to taste with salt and pepper.

5. Add the white wine to the skillet after adding the butter and allowing it to melt. Cook until the wine has decreased, about 2 to 3 minutes more.

6. Add the heavy cream and boil for a further two minutes, or until the sauce starts to get slightly thicker.

7. Take the wild mushroom feast off the stove and serve it over rice or pasta as a side dish.

Nutrition: Calories: 200 Fat: 15g Carbs: 8g Protein: 5g

NOTES:

_____

_____

_____

All the flavors of a loaded baked potato in soup form.

A rich and earthy soup made with a variety of wild mushrooms.

Prep time; Ten minutes

Cook Time; One hour

Serves; 4

Ingredients:

- Four large potatoes
- Two tbsp. of olive oil
- One tsp. of salt
- One-half tsp. of black pepper
- One-half cup of sour cream
- One-half cup of shredded cheddar cheese
- One-fourth cup of chopped green onions
- Four slices cooked bacon, crumbled

Directions:

1. Get the oven up to temperature, preferably 400F (200C).

2. Pat the potatoes dry and clean.

3. Make a few holes in each potato with a fork.

4. Season the potatoes with salt, pepper, and olive oil.

5. Put the potatoes straight onto the oven rack and bake for 1 hour, or until a fork inserted into them comes out soft.

6. Take the potatoes out of the oven and give them a little time to cool.

7. Cut each potato in half lengthwise, then use a fork to fluff the insides.

8. Sprinkle sour cream, cheddar cheese, green onions, and crumbled bacon over the top of each potato.

9. Serve immediately.

Nutrition: Calories: 425 Fat: 20g Carbs: 51g Protein: 12g

NOTES:

_____

_____

_____

A delightful combination of shrimp, corn, and a creamy broth.

Prep time; Ten minutes

Cook Time; Twenty minutes

Serves; 4

Ingredients:

- One lb (450g) shrimp, peeled and deveined
- Two cups corn kernels (fresh or frozen)
- One red bell pepper, diced
- One small onion, diced
- Three cloves of minced garlic
- One tbsp. olive oil
- One tsp. paprika
- One-half tsp. chili powder
- Pepper and salt to taste
- Fresh parsley (chopped) (as a garnish)

Directions:

1. In a large skillet, melt the olive oil over medium heat.

2. throw in some onions and peppers and let them soften in the pan for about four minutes.

3. Wait a full minute after adding the minced garlic before serving.

4. Add the shrimp to the skillet and cook for 2 to 3 minutes on each side, or until they are pink and opaque. After taking the shrimp out of the skillet, set it aside.

5. Cook the corn kernels in the same skillet for 5 minutes, stirring now and again.

6. Add the chili powder, paprika, salt, and pepper to the skillet and toss to evenly cover the corn. Add two more minutes of cooking.

7. Return the cooked shrimp to the skillet and cook it for an additional 2-3 minutes.

8. Turn off the heat and add some fresh parsley as a garnish.

Nutrition: Calories: 250 Fat: 5g Carbs: 25g Protein: 25g

NOTES:

_____

_____

_____

A comforting gluten-free soup with chicken and rice.

Prep time; Ten minutes

Cook Time; Thirty minutes

Serves; 4

Ingredients:

- Two boneless, skinless chicken breasts
- One cup white rice (gluten-free)
- Two cups chicken broth (gluten-free)
- One onion, diced
- Two cloves of minced garlic
- One tbsp. of olive oil
- One tsp. of dried thyme
- One tsp. of dried rosemary
- Pepper and salt to taste

Directions:

1. Olive oil should be heated in a large pot set over medium heat. When the onion and garlic have softened and released their aroma, they're ready to be added to the simmering pot.

2. Chop the chicken breasts into small pieces and incorporate them into the saucepan. Cook until every side is browned.

3. Fill the saucepan with the white rice, chicken stock, salt, pepper, and dried thyme and rosemary. Mix thoroughly to blend.

4. Reduce the heat, cover the pot, and maintain a simmer once the mixture has come to a boil. Keep at a low simmer for about 20 minutes, or until the rice is done and the chicken is fork-tender.

5. Take off from the heat and let it a five-minute rest before serving.

Nutrition: Calories: 320 Fat: 8g Carbs: 35g Protein: 25g

NOTES:

_____

_____

_____

A vegan-friendly soup brimming with lentils and colorful vegetables.

Prep time; Fifteen minutes

Cook Time; Forty minutes

Serves; 4

Ingredients:

- One cup of green lentils, rinsed
- Two cups of vegetable broth
- One chopped of onion
- Three cloves of minced garlic
- One red bell pepper, chopped
- One zucchini, chopped
- One eggplant, chopped
- One carrot, chopped
- One can diced tomatoes
- Two tbsp. tomato paste
- One tsp. of cumin
- One tsp. of paprika
- One-half tsp. turmeric
- Salt & pepper, as required

Directions:

1. Start a large pot of vegetable broth boiling. Add the lentils 15 minutes before they are done cooking and continue simmering. Empty and place aside.

2. Heat some oil in a different pan and sauté the garlic and onion until aromatic.

3. Include the carrot, bell pepper, eggplant, and zucchini in the pan. Cook till just beginning to soften.

4. Tomato paste, diced tomatoes, paprika, cumin, turmeric, salt, and pepper should all be added. Cook for 5 minutes.

5. Stir thoroughly after adding the cooked lentils to the vegetable mixture. Simmer for a further 10 minutes to give the flavors time to blend.

6. Present the hot Vegan Lentil and Veggie Feast accompanied by a crusty bread or rice side dish.

Nutrition (per serving): Calories: 320 Fat: 2g Carbs: 62g Protein: 18g

A heart-healthy minestrone with reduced sodium.

Prep time; Fifteen minutes

Cook Time; Forty-five minutes

Serves; 4

Ingredients:

- One tbsp. olive oil
- One medium chopped of onion
- Two cloves of minced garlic
- Two carrots, diced
- Two celery stalks, diced
- One zucchini, diced
- One yellow squash, diced
- One (15-ounce) can low-sodium diced tomatoes
- Four cups low-sodium vegetable broth
- One cup of water
- One tsp. of dried oregano
- One tsp. of dried basil
- One-half tsp. dried thyme
- One-half tsp. of salt
- One-fourth tsp. of black pepper
- One (Fifteen-ounce) can low-sodium kidney beans, rinsed and drained
- One cup whole wheat elbow pasta
- Two cups of chopped fresh spinach
- Parmesan cheese, grated (optional)

Directions:

1. Over medium heat, warm the olive oil in a big pot.

2. For around 5 minutes, soften the onion and garlic in oil.

3. Include the yellow squash, zucchini, carrots, and celery. Cook for a another 5 minutes, stirring now and then.

4. Put in the tomato sauce, vegetable broth, and water. Pepper, salt, thyme, basil, and oregano are added.

5. The soup should be brought to a boil, then reduced to a simmer for 30 minutes.

6. Include the spaghetti and kidney beans. Cook the pasta for a further 10 to 15 minutes, or until it is soft.

7. Add the chopped spinach and simmer, stirring, until wilted, 1-2 minutes.

8. If preferred, top the hot Low-Sodium Minestrone Bliss with shredded Parmesan cheese.

Nutrition: Calories: 240 Fat: 4g Carbs: 42g Protein: 10g

NOTES:

_____

_____

_____

A creamy tomato soup without the dairy, perfect for lactose-intolerant individuals.

Prep time; Ten minutes

Cook Time; Thirty minutes

Serves; 4

Ingredients:

- Two tbsp. of olive oil
- One diced onion
- Two cloves of minced garlic
- One can (14 oz) diced tomatoes
- One can (14 oz) coconut milk
- One tbsp. of tomato paste
- One tsp. of dried basil
- One tsp. of dried oregano
- Pepper and salt to taste

Directions:

1. Olive oil should be heated over medium heat in a large skillet. Cook the onion until it is translucent, then add the minced garlic.

2. Fill the pan with chopped tomatoes, tomato paste, coconut milk, dried oregano, dried basil, and salt and pepper. Mix thoroughly to blend.

3. Simmer for about 20 minutes, or until the flavors meld and the sauce thickens, after adding the ingredients.

4. Process the sauce in a conventional blender or an immersion blender until it's smooth and creamy.

5. Adjust seasonings if needed and serve hot over your favorite pasta or as a sauce for any other dish.

Nutrition (per serving): Calories: 210 Fat: 18g Carbs: 9g Protein: 3g

NOTES:

_____
_____
_____

A paleo-friendly soup featuring the sweetness of butternut squash.

Prep time; Fifteen minutes

Cook Time; Forty-five minutes

Serves; 4

Ingredients:

- One medium butternut squash
- Two tbsp. of olive oil
- One tsp. of ground cinnamon
- One-half tsp. of ground nutmeg
- One-half tsp. of sea salt
- One-fourth cup pure maple syrup
- One-fourth cup chopped pecans
- One-fourth cup dried cranberries

Directions:

1. Set the oven temperature to 400°F, or 200°C.

2. Remove the seeds from the butternut squash by slicing it in half lengthwise. After peeling, chop the squash into bite-sized cubes.

3. Combine the sea salt, nutmeg, cinnamon, and olive oil in a bowl and toss to coat the butternut squash cubes equally.

4. Spread the seasoned squash out in a single layer on a baking pan.

5. Roast the squash for 35 to 40 minutes, or until it's soft and has a light brown color, in a preheated oven. To guarantee uniform cooking, stir from time to time.

6. Take the squash out of the oven and pour some maple syrup over it. To coat, gently toss.

7. Top the squash with chopped pecans and dried cranberries.

8. To give the flavors time to combine, put the baking sheet back in the oven for a further five minutes.

9. Take it out of the oven and let it to cool down a little before serving.

Nutrition: Calories: 230 Fat: 10g Carbs: 35g Protein: 3g

NOTES:

_____

_____

_____

A spicy and hearty soup with sausage and beans.

Prep time; Fifteen minutes

Cook Time; Thirty minutes

Serves; 4

Ingredients:

- One lb spicy sausage, casings removed
- One diced of onion
- Two cloves of minced garlic
- One diced of red bell pepper
- One can (15 oz) kidney beans, rinsed and drained
- One can diced (15 oz) of tomatoes
- One cup chicken broth
- One tsp chili powder
- One-half tsp cumin
- Salt & pepper, as required
- Fresh cilantro, chopped (for garnish)
- Shredded cheese (optional, for serving)

Directions:

1. Brown the hot sausage over medium heat in a big skillet or Dutch oven. While cooking, break it up into little pieces with a wooden spoon.

2. Fill the skillet with the diced red bell pepper, diced onion, and minced garlic. Simmer the vegetables for an additional 5 minutes, or until they are tender.

3. Add the diced tomatoes, kidney beans, cumin, chili powder, chicken broth, salt, and pepper. Simmer the mixture for 15-20 minutes, stirring now and then.

4. Taste and, if necessary, adjust the seasoning. You can increase the amount of chili powder or cayenne pepper if you like your food hotter.

5. Serve the spicy sausage and bean warmth hot, garnished with chopped fresh cilantro. If you like, you can also add some shredded cheese on top.

Nutrition (per serving): Calories: 380 Fat: 22g Carbs: 21g Protein: 25g

NOTES:

_____

_____

_____

A refreshing chilled cucumber soup, ideal for hot days.

Prep time; Fifteen minutes

Cook Time; No Cooking Time Required

Serves; 4

Ingredients:

- Two English cucumbers
- One-half cup Greek yogurt
- One tbsp. fresh dill, chopped
- One tbsp. fresh mint, chopped
- One tbsp. lemon juice
- Salt & pepper, as required

Directions:

1. Start by peeling the cucumbers and cutting them into thin slices.

2. Add the Greek yogurt, lemon juice, mint, dill, and pepper to a mixing bowl.

3. Gently stir the yogurt mixture into the cucumber slices, tossing them until thoroughly covered.

4. Put the bowl inside the fridge for at least an hour to chill. Wrap it up.

5. Serve the chilled cucumber elegance as a refreshing side dish or appetizer.

Nutrition: Calories: 80 Fat: 2g Carbs: 12g Protein: 5g

NOTES:

_____

_____

_____

A German-inspired soup with cabbage and savory sausages.

Prep time; Fifteen minutes

Cook Time; Forty-five minutes

Serves; 4

Ingredients:

- One pound smoked sausage, sliced
- One small shredded head of cabbage
- One thinly sliced onion
- Two cloves of minced garlic
- Two tbsp. butter
- One tsp. caraway seeds
- Salt & pepper, as required
- One cup chicken broth
- One tbsp. apple cider vinegar

Directions:

1.Butter needs to be melted in a large skillet over medium heat.

2. Add the sausage slices and simmer for about 5 minutes, or until browned.

3. Take out and place aside the sausage from the griddle.

4. Put the onion slices and garlic mince in the same pan. Keep simmering until the onion is soft, about three minutes.

5. Shredded cabbage should wilt in a skillet for about 5 minutes over medium heat.

6. Add the pepper, salt, and caraway seeds. Mix thoroughly to blend.

7. Add the apple cider vinegar and chicken broth. Mix well to blend.

8. Simmer the cabbage for 30 minutes, covered, or until it is soft.

9. Add the cooked sausage back to the skillet and give it a quick swirl.

10. Cook the sausage for a further five minutes to reheat it.

11. Serve hot and enjoy!

Nutrition: Calories: 320 Fat: 20g Carbs: 8g Protein: 26g

A classic comfort food soup with tender chicken and dumplings.

Prep time; Twenty minutes

Cook Time; One hour

Serves; 4

Ingredients:

- One whole chicken, cut into pieces
- Two cups of all-purpose flour
- One-half tsp. of baking powder
- One-half tsp. of salt
- One-third cup of shortening
- One cup milk
- Four cups chicken broth
- Two cups frozen mixed vegetables
- Salt & pepper, as required

Directions:

1. Bring a big saucepan of water to a boil, then add the chicken pieces. After cooking the chicken for 45 minutes over low heat, it should be fully done. The chicken should be removed from the pan and allowed to cool. Set aside the chicken stock.

2. Flour, baking powder, and salt should be sifted together. Reduce the mixture's volume by cutting in the shortening until it resembles coarse crumbs. Stirring constantly, gradually add the milk until a soft dough forms.

3. Roll out the dough to a thickness of about 1/8 inch on a surface dusted with flour. Cut into dumplings or little squares.

4. Bring the chicken broth that was set aside to a boil in the pot. Add the dumplings and heat until they are soft and cooked through, about 15 minutes.

5. Shred the cooked chicken into bite-sized pieces, discarding the skin and bones, while the dumplings are cooking.

6. Combine the cooked dumplings in a pot with the shredded chicken, frozen mixed vegetables, salt, and pepper. Simmer the vegetables for ten more minutes, or until they are thoroughly cooked.

7. Present heated and savor!

Nutrition: Calories: 389 Fat: 14g Carbs: 42g Protein: 23g

A Mediterranean-inspired soup with chickpeas and fresh herbs.

Prep time; Fifteen minutes

Cook Time; Twenty-five minutes

Serves; 4

Ingredients:

- Two cans of chickpeas, drained and rinsed
- One diced of red bell pepper
- One diced of cucumber
- One finely chopped small red onion
- One cup , halved cherry tomatoes
- One-half cup Kalamata olives, pitted and halved
- One-fourth cup chopped fresh parsley
- One-fourth cup fresh mint, chopped
- One-third cup feta cheese, crumbled
- Two tbsp. of extra virgin olive oil
- Two tbsp. of lemon juice
- Salt & pepper, as required

Directions:

1. In a large bowl, toss together the chickpeas, red bell pepper, cucumber, red onion, cherry tomatoes, Kalamata olives, parsley, and mint.

2. Combine the lemon juice, olive oil, salt, and pepper in a small bowl.

3. Drizzle the chickpea mixture with the dressing, tossing to coat thoroughly.

4. Crumble the feta cheese and sprinkle it on top of the salad.

5. To let the flavors melt together, serve right away or chill for an hour.

Nutrition: Calories: 320 Fat: 18g Carbs: 32g Protein: 9g

NOTES:

_____

_____

_____

A Thai-inspired red curry soup with a spicy kick.

Prep time; Fifteen minutes

Cook Time; Twenty minutes

Serves; 4

Ingredients:

- Two tbsp. vegetable oil
- One small onion, sliced
- Two cloves of minced garlic
- Two tbsp. Thai red curry paste
- One bell pepper, sliced
- One carrot, julienned
- One zucchini, sliced
- One cup mushrooms, sliced
- One can coconut milk
- One cup vegetable broth
- Two tbsp. soy sauce
- One tbsp. brown sugar
- One lime, juiced
- One-half cup fresh basil leaves
- One-fourth cup fresh cilantro, chopped
- One-fourth cup peanuts, crushed

Directions:

1. Vegetable oil should be heated over medium heat in a big skillet. Cook the onions and garlic until they release their aroma.

2. Stir-fry the Thai red curry paste for one minute after adding it.

3. Include the mushrooms, zucchini, bell pepper, and carrot in the pan. The vegetables should be stir-fried for a few minutes to make them somewhat soft.

4. Add the brown sugar, soy sauce, coconut milk, and vegetable broth. After bringing to a simmer, cook the vegetables for 10 minutes or so, or until they are tender.

5. Add the cilantro, basil, and lime juice and stir. Simmer for one more minute.

6. Serve the Thai red curry over steamed rice or noodles. Top with crushed peanuts for extra crunch.

Nutrition (per serving): Calories: 350 Fat: 25g Carbs: 30g Protein: 8g

A southwestern-inspired soup served in edible tortilla bowls.

Prep time; Fifteen minutes

Cook Time; Twenty-five minutes

Serves; 4

Ingredients:

- One pound boneless, skinless chicken breasts, thinly sliced
- One tbsp. of olive oil
- One tsp. of chili powder
- One-half tsp. of cumin
- One-half tsp. of paprika
- One-half tsp. of garlic powder
- Salt & pepper, as required
- Four cups of cooked brown rice
- One cup black beans, drained and rinsed
- One cup of corn kernels
- One sliced of avocado
- One-half cup cherry tomatoes, halved
- One-fourth cup chopped cilantro
- Lime wedges for serving

Directions:

1. Olive oil should be heated in a large skillet over medium heat.

2. Add salt, pepper, chili powder, cumin, paprika, and garlic powder to the chicken breasts.

3. When the chicken is no longer pink in the middle, add it to the skillet and cook for another 6-8 minutes on each side.

4. Before slicing into strips, take the cooked chicken out of the skillet and let it a few minutes to rest.

5. In each serving bowl, layer 1 cup of cooked brown rice, One-fourth cup black beans, One-fourth cup corn kernels, sliced avocado, cherry tomato halves, and sliced chicken.

6. Lastly, garnish with chopped cilantro and lime wedges.

Nutrition: Calories: 500 Fat: 12g Carbs: 60g Protein: 39g

NOTES:

_____
_____
_____

A creamy soup featuring cauliflower and sharp cheddar cheese.

Prep time; Ten minutes

Cook Time; Twenty-five minutes

Serves; 4

Ingredients:

- One large cut into florets head of cauliflower
- Two tbsp. butter
- Two tbsp. all-purpose flour
- One cup of milk
- One cup of shredded cheddar cheese
- To taste, salt and pepper

Directions:

1. Cook the cauliflower florets in a big pot of boiling water for about 5 minutes, or until they are crisp-tender. Empty and place aside.

2. Butter should be melted in the same pan over low to medium heat. Mix the flour in with a whisk.

3. Slowly pour in the milk while continuously whisking. Warm the sauce over low heat until it thickens, about two to three minutes.

4. Add the shredded cheddar cheese to the sauce and turn the heat down to low. Once the sauce is smooth and the cheese has melted, stir.

5. Add salt and pepper to taste as needed.

6. Return the cooked cauliflower and cheese sauce to the pot. To evenly coat the cauliflower, gently stir.

7. Cook to a thoroughly heated through, 2 to 3 minutes more.

8. You may serve the creamy cauliflower and cheddar as an appetizer or entrée.

Nutrition: Calories: 220 Fat: 15g Carbs: 9g Protein: 12g

NOTES:

_____
_____
_____

A vegan-friendly twist on classic split pea soup.

Prep time; Ten minutes

Cook Time; One hour and thirty minutes

Serves; 4

Ingredients:

- One cup of dried split peas
- One chopped of onion
- Two cloves of minced garlic
- Two carrots, diced
- Two celery stalks, diced
- Four cups vegetable broth
- One tsp. dried thyme
- One bay leaf
- Salt & pepper, as required
- Fresh parsley, chopped (for garnish)

Directions:

1. In a large saucepan, melt some oil over moderate heat. Put in the vegetables, onion, garlic, and celery. For about 5 minutes, or until tender, simmer the vegetables.2. Add the rinsed split peas to the pot. Mix well with the veggies.

3. Season the vegetable stock with salt, pepper, thyme, and a bay leaf. Bring to a boil, then reduce heat to low, and simmer for 1 hour, or until split peas are mushy and cooked through.

4. Remove the bay leaf and purée the soup in a regular or immersion blender until it reaches a creamy consistency.

5. Taste and, if necessary, adjust seasonings.

6. Garnish with fresh parsley and serve hot.

Nutrition: Calories: 250 Fat: 1g Carbs: 50g Protein: 15g

NOTES:

_____

_____

_____

A Moroccan-spiced soup with lentils and chickpeas.

Prep time; Ten minutes

Cook Time; Thirty minutes

Serves; 4

Ingredients:

- One cup dried lentils
- One cup chickpeas
- One chopped of onion
- Three cloves of minced garlic
- One carrot, diced
- One celery stalk, diced
- One red bell pepper, diced
- One tbsp. of olive oil
- One tsp. of cumin
- One tsp. of paprika
- One tsp. of turmeric
- One tsp. of ground coriander
- One tsp. ground cinnamon
- Two cups vegetable broth
- One can diced tomatoes
- Salt & pepper, as required
- Fresh cilantro, chopped (for garnish)

Directions:

1. Rinse the lentils and chickpeas under cold water, then soak them separately in water for about 2 hours. Drain and set aside.

2. In a big saucepan over medium heat, olive oil should be warmed. Mince the garlic and dice the onion, then sauté them together until the garlic is fragrant and the onion is lightly browned.

3. Include the red bell pepper, celery, and chopped carrot in the pot. Vegetables need about 5 minutes of cooking time to start softening.

4. Fill the saucepan with the soaked lentils, soaked chickpeas, turmeric, coriander, cumin, and paprika. Coat the vegetables and beans in the spices by giving them a good stir.

5. Add the diced tomatoes and veggie broth. Once again, stir, and then increase the heat to a boil. After lowering the heat to low and covering the pot, cook the lentils and chickpeas until they are soft, about 30 minutes.

6. You can season to taste with salt and pepper. You can thin out the mixture by adding extra water or vegetable broth if it seems too thick.

7. Serve the Moroccan lentil and chickpea stew hot, garnished with fresh chopped cilantro. It can be enjoyed on its own or served over steamed rice or couscous.

Nutrition: Calories: 250 Fat: 4g Carbs: 44g Protein: 14g

NOTES:

_____

_____

_____

A Japanese noodle soup with thick udon noodles.

Prep time; Ten minutes

Cook Time; Fifteen minutes

Serves; 2

Ingredients:

- 200g udon noodles
- Two cups vegetable broth
- Two tbsp.of soy sauce
- One tbsp. mirin
- One tbsp. sesame oil
- One sliced of onion
- Two cloves of minced garlic
- One carrot, julienned
- One red bell pepper, sliced
- One cup mushrooms, sliced
- One cup baby spinach

Directions:

1. Prepare the udon noodles per the directions on the package. Empty and place aside.

2. Heat the sesame oil in a large saucepan over low to medium heat. To release their flavor, cook the onions and garlic.

3. Include the bell pepper, mushrooms, and carrot; sauté until soft.

4. Add the mirin, soy sauce, and vegetable broth. After bringing to a boil, lower heat, and simmer for five minutes.

5. Put the cooked udon noodles and baby spinach in the pot. Continue cooking for another two to three minutes, stirring regularly, or until the spinach is wilted.

6. Take the Udon Noodle Euphoria soup off the stove and serve it hot.

Nutrition (per serving): Calories: 300 Fat: 5g Carbs: 55g Protein: 10g

NOTES:

_____

_____

_____

A robust soup with beef and a variety of vegetables.

Prep time; Fifteen minutes

Cook Time; Forty-five minutes

Serves; 4

Ingredients:

- One lb beef (such as stew meat or sirloin), cut into cubes
- Two tbsp. olive oil
- One onion, diced
- Three cloves of minced garlic
- Two carrots, peeled and sliced
- Two celery stalks, sliced
- One bell pepper, diced
- One zucchini, diced
- One can (14.5 oz) diced tomatoes
- One cup beef broth
- One tsp. of dried thyme
- One tsp. of dried rosemary
- Salt & pepper, as required

Directions:

1. In a large pot or Dutch oven, warm the olive oil over medium heat. After adding the meat cubes, sauté them until they are uniformly browned. Take the steak away from the heat and set it aside.

2. Put the onions and garlic in the same pan. The onion should be cooked until it is completely clear. Put in the vegetables: pepper, zucchini, carrots, and celery. Stir the mixture occasionally and let it cook for 5 minutes.

3. Put the beef back in the saucepan. Add the dried thyme, dried rosemary, diced tomatoes, beef broth, salt, and pepper. After bringing to a boil, turn down the heat. The beef should be tender after 30 minutes of simmering under cover.

4. Serve the beef and vegetable medley hot. Enjoy!

Nutrition: Calories: 350 Fat: 12g Carbs: 15g Protein: 40g

NOTES:

_____

_____

_____

A creamy soup infused with the warm flavors of pumpkin spice.

Prep time; Ten minutes

Cook Time; Twenty-five minutes

Serves; 4

Ingredients:

- One cup pumpkin puree
- One cup of milk
- One-half cup of heavy cream
- One-fourth cup of granulated sugar
- One tsp. pumpkin pie spice
- One-half tsp. of vanilla essence
- Whipped cream, for garnish
- Cinnamon powder, as a finishing touch

Directions:

1. Place the pumpkin puree, heavy cream, milk, sugar, and pumpkin pie spice in a saucepan. Mix thoroughly.

2. Turn the heat down to medium and simmer the mixture, stirring now and again. Allow to simmer until slightly thickened, about 20 minutes.

3. Turn off the heat and mix in the vanilla extract in the pot.

4. Allow the blend to reach room temperature.

5. After the mixture cools, pour it into a blender and process it until it's smooth.

6. After mixing all the ingredients together, pour them into serving glasses or plates and chill for at least 4 hours to set.

7. Add some whipped cream and ground cinnamon as garnish before serving.

Nutrition (per serving): Calories: 210 Fat: 14g Carbs: 20g Protein: 3g

NOTES:

_____

_____

_____

A spicy and tangy Chinese soup with tofu and mushrooms.

Prep time; Fifteen minutes

Cook Time; Twenty-five minutes

Serves; 4

Ingredients:

- One tbsp. vegetable oil
- One-half cup sliced mushrooms
- One-half cup of julienned carrots
- One-fourth cup of sliced bamboo shoots
- One-fourth cup sliced of water chestnuts
- One-fourth cup diced of tofu
- Four cups of vegetable broth or chicken broth
- Two tbsp. of soy sauce
- Two tbsp. rice vinegar
- One tsp. chili garlic sauce
- One-fourth tsp. ground white pepper
- One-fourth tsp. ground ginger
- Two tbsp. cornstarch
- Two tbsp. of water
- Two large eggs, lightly beaten
- Two green onions, sliced

Directions:

1. In a large saucepan, melt the vegetable oil over moderate heat.

2. Tofu, water chestnuts, bamboo shoots, mushrooms, and carrots should all be added to the saucepan and cooked together. It should take around 5 minutes to soften in the pan.

3. Add the ginger, white pepper, chili garlic sauce, soy sauce, rice vinegar, and broth. Simmer for ten minutes after bringing to a simmer.

4. In a small bowl, make a slurry out of the cornstarch and water. To adjust the soup's consistency, add the slurry gradually while stirring frequently.

5. After the soup has thickened, stir the soup gently in one direction while gradually drizzling in the beaten eggs. Egg ribbons will result from this.

6. Remove the pot from heat and garnish with green onions.

7. Serve hot and savor!

Nutrition: (per serving) Calories: 180 Fat: 8g Carbs: 16g Protein: 12g

A hearty Tuscan soup with bread and vegetables.

Prep time; Twenty minutes

Cook Time; One hour and thirty minutes

Serves; 6

Ingredients:

- One cup dried cannellini beans
- Four tbsp. olive oil
- One finely chopped onion
- Two carrots, diced and peeled
- Two celery stalks, diced
- Three cloves of minced garlic
- One bunch of chopped kale
- One bunch Swiss chard, chopped
- One small head cabbage, shredded
- Four tomatoes, diced
- Four cups vegetable broth
- Two cups water
- One tsp. of dried thyme
- One tsp. of dried oregano
- Salt & pepper, as required
- Four slices day-old bread, toasted
- Parmesan cheese, grated (for serving)

Directions:

1. Let the dried cannellini beans soak for the entire night, then rinse and drain.

2. Two tablespoons of olive oil, in a big skillet, over medium heat. Prepare the celery, carrot, and onion by sautéing them until they are tender.

3. Cook for a further minute after adding the minced garlic.

4. Add the cabbage, Swiss chard, and kale. Simmer until tender.

5. Stir in the tomatoes, water, vegetable broth, soaked beans, dried oregano, thyme, and pepper. Heat till boiling.

6. Lower the heat and boil the soup until the beans are soft, about 1 hour.

7. Use a potato masher or the back of a spoon to crush some of the beans and thicken the soup.

8. After toasting, smear the bread pieces with garlic. Put a single piece of bread at the base of every serving bowl.

9. Spoon hot soup onto bread and dress with the leftover olive oil.

10. Grate some fresh Parmesan cheese over the top and serve.

Nutrition: Calories: 250 Fat: 10g Carbs: 30g Protein: 10g

NOTES:

_____

_____

_____

A Greek-inspired soup with lemony chicken and orzo.

Prep time; Fifteen minutes

Cook Time; One hour

Serves; 4

Ingredients:

- Four chicken breasts, bone-in, skin-on
- One-fourth cup olive oil
- Three cloves of minced garlic
- Two lemons, juiced and zested
- One tsp. of dried oregano
- One tsp. of dried thyme
- One-half tsp. of salt
- One-fourth tsp. of black pepper
- One-half cup of chicken broth

Directions:

1. Turn the oven on to 375°F, or 190°C.

2. Olive oil, garlic, lemon zest, lemon juice, oregano, thyme, salt, and pepper should be mixed together in a small bowl.

3. Transfer the marinade to a baking sheet and cover the chicken breasts. Ensure that the chicken has a good coating.

4. In a preheated oven, bake the chicken for 45 minutes, or until it reaches an internal temperature of 165 degrees F and a golden brown color. Every fifteen minutes, baste the chicken with the marinade.

5. Before serving, The chicken needs to rest for 5 minutes after being removed from the oven.

6. Optional: Squeeze extra lemon juice over the chicken before serving.

7. Serve the Greek Lemon Chicken with your favorite side dishes.

Nutrition: Calories: 320 Fat: 18g Carbs: 4g Protein: 36g

NOTES:

_____

_____

_____

Conclusion

Thank you for making it to the end. crafting a successful soup cookbook requires a combination of creativity, knowledge, and attention to detail. Throughout the process, it is important to keep the target audience in mind and strive to create a collection of recipes that cater to their taste preferences and dietary requirements.

To begin, it is essential to conduct thorough research on various soup recipes, ensuring the inclusion of both classic favorites and innovative creations. Experimenting with different ingredients and flavors can help add a unique touch to the cookbook and make it stand out among others.

One important tip is to provide clear and concise instructions for every recipe. Not everyone is an experienced cook, so it's crucial to explain each step in a way that is easy to understand. Adding photographs or illustrations can also be helpful, providing visual guidance for readers.

Another aspect to consider is the use of seasonal ingredients. Incorporating fresh produce that is readily available during specific times of the year can enhance the flavor and nutritional value of the soups. It also adds variety to the cookbook, allowing readers to explore different ingredients throughout the seasons.

Additionally, including a section on soup garnishes and accompaniments can elevate the overall dining experience. Suggesting toppings, such as croutons, cheese, or herbs, can provide readers with ideas for enhancing the presentation and taste of their soups.

A well-organized index is vital to facilitate easy navigation through the cookbook. Categorizing soups based on themes, flavors, or dietary restrictions can aid readers in quickly finding recipes that suit their preferences or dietary needs. It's also beneficial to include a table of contents and page numbers for easy reference.

Lastly, promoting interaction with readers is crucial for any cookbook. Encouraging them to share their soup creations on social media platforms using a unique hashtag or offering a dedicated website for users to connect and exchange feedback can create a sense of community around the cookbook.

A successful soup cookbook combines a diverse range of recipes, clear instructions, seasonal ingredients, toppings suggestions, an organized index, and reader engagement. By implementing these tips, aspiring authors can create a soup cookbook that is not only informative but also inspiring, ensuring that readers are eager to try out a variety of flavorful soups in their own kitchens.

I hope you liked this book!

Printed in Great Britain
by Amazon

34460378R00064